Rosey Grier's
All-American Heroes

ROSEY GRIER'S
ALL-AMERICAN
★ HEROES ★

Multicultural Success Stories

ROOSEVELT "ROSEY" GRIER

MasterMedia Limited · New York

Published by MasterMedia Limited.

MASTERMEDIA and colophon are registered
trademarks of MasterMedia Limited.

Library of Congress Cataloging-in-Publication Data
Grier, Rosey
    [All-American heroes]
    Rosey Grier's All-American heroes : multicultural success stories /
    Roosevelt "Rosey" Grier
        p.   cm.
    ISBN 0-942361-63-6
    1. Minorities—United States—Biography.   2. Success—United
States.   3. Minorities—United States—Biography.   I. Title.
    E184.A1G88   1993
    305.5'6'092273—dc20
    [B]   92–37761
                                                                    CIP

Manufactured in the United States of America
Designed by Jacqueline Schuman
Production services by Martin Cook Associates, New York

10 9 8 7 6 5 4 3 2 1

Contents

David S. Bernstein

Black, Jewish, and conservative, David S. Bernstein is using his pen to rock conventional political wisdom. As founding editor of *Diversity and Division: A Critical Journal of Race and Culture,* the 26-year-old intellectual firebrand is challenging America's status quo from every angle imaginable.

Tony Brown

Growing up poor during the Depression in segregated Charleston, West Virginia, Tony Brown learned he wouldn't get anything in life he wasn't willing to work for. Now, as a prominent black journalist with his own long-running public television show, Brown preaches his credo of self-help as a path out of poverty for all African-Americans.

Roscoe Bunn

A rebellious teenager, Roscoe Bunn loved racing cars more than school, so he dropped out of college. Then he got drafted, and the horrors of war in Vietnam convinced him to make something of his life. Today he's a successful business executive with one of America's largest companies.

Ben Nighthorse Campbell

Ben Nighthorse Campbell definitely isn't your average politician. A Cheyenne renegade, rancher, judo master, and renowned Indian jewelry designer, Campbell was perhaps the only congressman to ever require special approval to wear his clothes in the hallowed U.S. House of Representatives. Now, as the first native American elected to the U.S. Senate, Campbell plans to maintain his unique sartorial style, promising voters that being a Senator won't turn him into another "three-piece suiter."

she was a fierce advocate in the civil rights movement. Today, as founder and president of the Children's Defense Fund, Edelman is a determined voice for America's disadvantaged kids.

Many high school dropouts don't make it back to the classroom. But Joseph Fernandez did. He not only finished high school, he also earned a doctorate degree in education. Today, as chancellor of New York City's public schools, he's running the very system he dropped out of.

George C. Fraser believes that one of the best ways for blacks to succeed is to learn from each other. That's why he created *Success-Guides,* professional directories designed to link black professionals across the country and ultimately, Fraser hopes, around the world.

As a newlywed and young mother, Johnnie Mae Gibson got a job with a police department in Georgia to help pay the bills. She never dreamed it was the first step toward breaking barriers for black women in law enforcement. Gibson eventually became one of the first black women ever hired as a special agent with the FBI.

For generations, Paula Giddings's family revered education as the path to a better life. But the racism Giddings encountered in the classroom turned her away from academia for years. Now the editor and writer is back in the classroom—this time as a professor and critical thinker on the impact racism and sexism have on African-American women.

One of the few men in America willing to be seen by millions in nothing but his underwear, Karl Hampton isn't afraid to take a chance. He grew up picking cotton in rural Mississippi. Now he represents the U.S. government as an agricultural economist working with countries around the world.

Yvonne Jackson knows what it's like to be different from society's mainstream. As a black woman she's faced down racism and sexism, and managed to build a highly successful business career. Now she's drawing on her experiences to help open doors for a new wave of minorities, immigrants, and women seeking their own success in corporate America.

Dedication

A special thanks to:

* Diane Graham for bringing Susan Stautberg and myself together

* all the people who helped make this book possible

* friends and family, especially Margie, Little Rosey, Cheryl, Keith, Kimberly, Alan, James, Eula, Alice, Evan, Butler, William, Sam, Rufus, Willy B., Sammy Lee, Joyleonard, Freddie, and Robert

Preface

The face of America is changing. More than at any other time in our history, we are a land of many races. People from all kinds of backgrounds are making important contributions and holding prominent positions in politics and business, art and education.

Traditionally America has been called a melting pot. Today, it is often described as a mosaic because of the immigrants we attract from all corners of the world. In the 1980s alone, 8.7 million people poured into this country, hungry for opportunity and a better life.

Like many Americans, I am watching this new population wave with a mixture of admiration and concern—admiration for the courage it takes to put down roots in a new land, and concern because I can appreciate the obstacles these people will face when they try to integrate into a new culture.

The diversity immigrants bring can be a powerful force in shaping the future of our country. But for many, especially new immigrants and their children, the first generation to be born on U.S. soil, the American dream is just that—a dream. They are confronted with racial prejudice, sometimes poverty, and practical problems, such as learning another language. Often, their lives are a day-to-day struggle that they survive through sheer will and a determination to succeed. Those who make it usually do so with the support of people who care enough to show them the way, to teach them how to build the better life they came to America to find.

I understand the challenge of overcoming obstacles such as prejudice and poverty. As a black man raised in rural Georgia, the son of uneducated sharecroppers, I never imagined that one day I'd be a professional football star or become friends with a U.S. President.

Realizing my dreams took a lot of hard work and determination. And I thank God every day for what I've been able to achieve. But I also was very lucky to have people, beginning with my parents, who encouraged me, believed in me, and maybe most importantly, helped me stay on course, even when I stumbled. When I think back on my life, those people are my heroes — without them, I can honestly say, I might not be where I am today.

That's why I wanted to do this book. Because we all need heroes — especially when we're young or just starting out on a new life. And because the face of America is changing so rapidly, I was particularly interested in men and women from different ethnic backgrounds, experiences, and professions who could serve as role models.

I'm happy to say I found many successful people who agreed to share their stories for this book. Because I wanted every person to bring their own special spirit to the project, the profiles do not follow a particular formula. At the same time, I did focus on some common themes. For example, I wanted to know whether there had been an event or circumstance that marked a turning point in their lives, and whether they could cite someone who clearly had been instrumental in setting them on their paths to success.

I also was curious about the kinds of obstacles they had faced, and more importantly, how they overcame those roadblocks. What qualities do successful people possess that enable them to push ahead — even when other people might be saying, "It can't be done"?

Success comes in many forms and, as the heroes here show, the measure of success is often a personal one. For many, the paths to the prestigious positions they hold today were paved with hardship and sometimes heartache. But even the sad stories are inspiring — because everyone in this book is a survivor with an important message to share.

Their willingness to open up their lives for public view, and to talk with such candor and concern for others who might follow in their footsteps, helped make this book not only possible, but also a real pleasure to produce.

So many have generously given their time and offered insights into their triumphs and mistakes that only they could have shared; such spirited involvement deserves a special thank-you — you helped give this book its heartbeat.

I also want to express my gratitude to the professionals whose behind-the-scenes efforts were essential to this project.

To Diana Lynn, whose dedication and editorial expertise kept this project on track, with the support of Christopher Turek's thorough research, and the creative talents of Alan Marks, Linda Morel, and Bonnie Kaufman in compiling the profiles.

And finally, a heartfelt thanks to my publisher, Susan Stautberg, for her inspiration and support throughout the process of bringing this book to print.

Introduction

 Life presents challenges to all of us — but every challenge is an opportunity to grow.

This book is about the heroes in America — women and men who have taken the talents God gave them and made something of their lives. Many of them found success by turning around a bad situation. And in some ways, that's the most satisfying success of all. But too often, I think, people feel they don't have a chance at a good life because they grew up on the wrong side of the tracks or were born at the wrong time. By believing this, they give themselves every reason to fail.

But I don't believe that, not for one minute. Every man and woman on this earth is born with a gift — a talent, a skill, or a quality that is unique to them. Some people realize what their gifts are, and they work hard to develop them and build meaningful, successful lives.

That's the kind of people you're going to meet in this book. Every hero has a different story, but in some ways, these people are all alike: they had the dedication to make their dreams come true. No one in this book was an overnight success — they all worked hard and suffered setbacks. As you will see from their stories, life is not a bed of roses — for anyone. But success is possible for everyone. All it takes is the right kind of commitment.

This book will show you all the good things that can happen to people when preparation meets opportunity. Often when successful people are asked about their lives, they say, "Well, I seized the opportunity."

I believe that success happens most often to people with the right mind-set who are doing everything humanly possible to develop their God-given abilities. That way, when opportunity comes, you can step in and do your part to achieve success. And sometimes that means daring to take a chance.

Certainly that's been true in my life.

I grew up in Georgia in a big family—I have eleven brothers and sisters. As a young boy, I had to work very hard in the fields. I remember shaking peanuts when I was only 5, and even when I started school I had to keep working to help support my family. My days began at dawn, and I often worked late into the evening to meet all my obligations.

But it was worth it to me, because I had this great desire to go to school and exercise my mind. Learning about new things excited me. But since I had to work so hard on the farm, a lot of times I didn't do all my homework. So I got whopped on the hand a lot by my teachers.

Things got a little bit better when my family moved to New Jersey. I was able to go to school. Still, I was not a brilliant student. But I never thought about failing—I just worked on never quitting. I was a stubborn kid who refused to give up.

One of the people who helped me through that time was a lady in my high school. Her name was Mrs. Spring, and what I remember most about her was how she just kept encouraging me to work hard. I was very shy about talking because of my Georgia accent, and my English was atrocious. But Mrs. Spring made me believe I could improve. "Rosey, you can do it," she said, "but you've just got to keep working." So I kept at it, and I graduated in the top fifth of my class.

That was one of my first experiences with success and the power of hard work. It also taught me about the importance of preparation. After graduation, I was offered twenty-six college scholarships. I visited many campuses, but I knew I'd found the right place when Penn State University told me that if I worked hard I could graduate from college. Unlike some of the other colleges, they hadn't tried to sell me on their athletic program alone—and that's what sold me on Penn State.

College was a real test of my determination. I remember sitting in class at the university, saying to myself, "Are you ever going to get out of here?" My first semester I almost flunked out. But I'd already proved to myself in high school that if I worked hard, I could succeed.

Roosevelt "Rosey" Grier

Still, I must tell you that when I found myself graduating from college, it seemed extraordinary to me. I never dreamed that I would be able to grow from a cotton-picker, peanut-shaker Georgia boy into a Penn State graduate.

After college, I went into professional football and had a very successful career with the New York Giants and the Los Angeles Rams. I had the opportunity to play in five NFL championship games with the Giants.

But even as I was experiencing this success, I had things in my life

I wanted to work on. I still had a great fear of talking, even though in college I had forced myself to take speech classes where I had to get up and talk extemporaneously. I could talk about football and things that I knew about, but I felt my intellectual range was narrow, and I was never satisfied that I had been able to say the things that were in my heart.

All that changed when I met Bobby Kennedy while working on a telethon to raise money for inner city kids. I went over to the Kennedys' home and I just loved the family right off the bat, and they liked me. When Bobby decided to run for the presidency, I joined his campaign. Often on the campaign trail, he would invite me to the microphone to make a speech. This terrified me, so I'd go up to the microphone and say, "My name is Rosey Grier, and I'm glad to be here." And then I'd sit down quickly.

Then one day I got a call from Bobby's brother-in-law, Steven Smith, who was supposed to be making a speech about Bobby at the Brentwood Country Club. He couldn't go to the meeting, and wanted me to fill in for him. Well, I was very nervous about speaking at this exclusive club because all the members were white and wealthy. But Steven reminded me that I had promised to help Bobby get elected.

So I went, and many famous people spoke that day, celebrities like Warren Beatty, Raquel Welch, and Shelley Winters. They were eloquent, so you can imagine how I felt when they said, "Rosey, you're up next."

I went to the microphone and said, "Well, I'm not with these folks. But if I had you all on a football field, I could drive you right to the dirt." That got a laugh, which encouraged me, so I proceeded to share my dreams for America. I felt compelled to speak from my heart, because that was the only way I could talk about Bobby Kennedy—the man I respected, the man I loved, and the man I wanted to be President. By sharing who I was, and giving the audience a real picture of myself and what I believed in, I finally broke through the barrier that had made me so afraid to talk in public.

I continued to be a part of Bobby's campaign because we both had dreams for America. But those dreams were shattered when Sirhan Sirhan shot Bobby at a political gathering. I tried to save

Bobby by throwing myself on Sirhan and grabbing the gun, but only succeeded in saving Sirhan from being massacred by the angry crowd. When Bobby died from that gunshot, something in me died, too.

I was devastated and it took a long while to get back on my feet. I went through a depression, got divorced, and even retired from football. My life was a mess until I met some gang kids whom no one wanted because they had killed a three-year-old girl. I started working with those kids and discovered something about myself. Though I had achieved much success and I was a well-known guy—by that point in my life, I'd also made movies and had my own television show—I had no foundation under me, no hopes and dreams on which to build my life. I felt that when people looked at me what they saw was a big, powerful black guy; but on the inside, I felt like a little kid looking for answers.

I started to find my answers after I met a woman named Ann Ludick, who told me about a fellow who taught the Bible on television. I began to watch him and my life changed. I made the decision to accept Christ, and today I am an ordained minister.

Since becoming a Christian, I've committed my life to helping others. I've been involved in a number of programs and projects to improve the lives of America's underprivileged, young and old. In particular, I'm dedicated to saving the inner city through my work with "Are You Committed?" This organization is focused on solving the problems—drugs, crime, racism, and unemployment, to name a few—that undermine urban communities and threaten the futures of young people who live there.

So, that's my story, and as you can see, my life has been a series of ups and downs. Like I said, being successful doesn't mean your life is a bed of roses. What matters is how you handle life's setbacks.

That's why I think you're going to enjoy meeting the people in this book. Every one of them has important lessons to share about determination, hard work, hope, and believing in yourself. No two stories are alike, but you will begin to see a pattern in their lives. Certain things are necessary for success, no matter who you are.

When asked what helped them succeed, the heroes offered this advice:

STAY IN SCHOOL

Education is the single most important thing you can do to prepare for your future. Today, many careers—even athletics—are closed to people who don't have a college degree. Education opens doors in ways you may not even imagine.

For one, education can be a great equalizer. This is particularly true if you, like me, are considered a minority. We often have to work extra hard to prove ourselves—to show people that being African-American or Puerto Rican or Indian doesn't affect our intelligence, our abilities, or our ambitions. And if you do encounter prejudice, education often forces people to be fair—because it's an objective measure of your ability to succeed.

General Colin Powell, chairman of the Joint Chiefs of Staff, takes every opportunity to talk with young people across the country about the importance of education. "You must finish high school," he tells them.

Dropping out only leads to dead ends, but "if you get your diploma, you are on your way to somewhere," Powell says.

Education not only gives you the training you may need to do a particular job, but it shows you're prepared to work hard to meet a goal.

Everyone in this book dreamed of going to college, and many of them made it—often by themselves because their parents couldn't afford to send them. Some of them had grades good enough to win scholarships; others held down jobs and even supported families while they pursued their degrees. Either way, they were determined to make that investment in themselves and their futures.

But however they got through college, and no matter how long it took them, the heroes all agree: don't kid yourself that education doesn't matter.

DARE TO DREAM

Some people just naturally seem to know what they want to do with their lives. Take Brady Keys, Jr. He was 8 when he decided he was going to be a football player and a businessman.

He's been both. After playing professional ball for several years, mostly with the Pittsburgh Steelers, he opened a restaurant. His business was so successful, he became the first black man to be a major restaurant franchiser. Today Keys is a self-made millionaire who uses his wealth and influence to help young people start their own businesses.

Journalist David S. Bernstein is another example. "From the time I was young, I was determined to do something 'special' with my life," he said. "When I was about 13 or 14 years old, I once told a group of adults that I was sure I would be famous someday. I didn't know what I would be doing, or how it would occur, but I truly believed that I would accomplish something of worth during my lifetime."

For others, finding success is more like a journey. They have a general idea of the direction they'd like to go in, but they're willing to explore along the way.

Daisy Chin-Lor zig-zagged her way to the top ranks of Avon Products by being willing to work in a lot of different departments and take on all kinds of responsibility. Now, as president of the company's highly competitive Taiwan business, Chin-Lor is often asked how she achieved such a prominent position early in her career.

"I feel I've been very fortunate," she said. "I was always open to new opportunities. If you hang your hat on a certain position, it might not be there when you're ready for it."

Part of what makes success fun is that there are many ways to find it. You must decide which approach works for you—no one can do that for you. Dreams are the foundation on which you build your success.

GO THE DISTANCE WITH GOALS

A wise person once said, "If you don't know where you're going, you might end up somewhere you don't want to be."

To me, that means setting goals. I think of goals as markers on the path to success—because they help you see how far you need to go, and how far you've already come.

Many people resist the idea of setting goals. They think it's too much work, or they're afraid—because a goal is like a promise you make to yourself.

It takes practice to set goals that are challenging enough to keep you excited but not so big you get overwhelmed just thinking about them. Goals help you make your dreams come true one step at a time.

Often the lives of successful people seem almost magical because good things just seem to come their way. You may have even heard the saying "He was in the right place at the right time." But in my experience, such luck is always preceded by a lot of hard work and a willingness to knock on a lot of doors before the right one opens.

TV executive George L. Miles, Jr., worked two decades to meet one of his goals. "Years ago, I decided that what I wanted to do most was contribute my fair share to my community," he said. "I got into public television because it serves the community in so many important ways."

Today Miles is head of WNET-TV in New York, the country's largest public television station. But his path to success took many twists and turns. When Miles first got out of college with an accounting degree, his goal was to get a job with a major firm—but it was the sixties, and blacks weren't being hired for such positions.

That didn't stop Miles from building the career he really wanted. "You can't just sit back and wait for something to happen," he said. "Only *you* can make it happen."

Goals not only help you measure your progress, they also can guide your choices along the way. If you haven't spent the time to figure out where you want your life to go you'll have a hard time trying to decide whether to seize any unexpected opportunity that crosses your path.

DON'T ACCEPT DEFEAT

Some of the most successful people in the world have been failures at one point or another in their lives. But they were not afraid to follow their hearts and build their dreams.

Spike Lee's first movie was never finished after he got into a dispute with the Screen Actors Guild. He lost $40,000 on that project, but he didn't lose his drive to make films. A year later, he made another movie in twelve days, on a paltry budget of $175,000— which he scraped together while he was still producing the film.

"We never knew where the next nickel was going to come from, so we wrote to or called everybody we knew in the world, asking them to send money, even if it was just $50," Lee said. "Each day while we were shooting, someone would go back to my house to see if any checks had come and then rush them to the bank, and we'd just hope they'd clear in time."

Determined people rarely fail.

The first time college freshman Karl Hampton walked into his chemistry class, the professor asked him if he was a football player. When Hampton, who was attending school on an athletic scholarship, said yes, the professor told him, "Then you might as well turn around and walk out that door right now, because you're going to flunk my class."

Not only did Hampton pass the class, he also made an *A* on every exam the teacher gave. "I think I kind of changed her opinion about football players," said Hampton, who's now an agricultural economist on an assignment in Brazil for the U.S. Department of Agriculture.

If you have a dream, hold on to it. Successful people are not afraid to take chances because they know even failure has its advantages. Even when things don't turn out quite right, you're still usually farther along than if you hadn't tried at all. Mistakes can teach you a lot, if you're willing to learn.

STAY IN TOUCH WITH YOUR SPIRITUAL SELF

Sometimes, no matter how hard you try, everything seems to go wrong. That's when it's helpful to have something you believe in that transcends the day-to-day events of your life. Some people connect with their spiritual self by meditating, others by spending time in nature. For me, and for many of the heroes in this book, religion is a great comfort in times of distress.

FBI Agent Johnnie Mae Gibson has faced discrimination and danger in her career, but she's always persevered because she believes "God put me on earth to be someone of significance, a highly important black female."

Whenever her problems feel unbearable, Gibson finds the strength to go on by meditating and quietly reading the Bible. "I truly believe that there is a guardian angel watching over me and keeping me out of harm," she said.

This book is not about religion, but many of my ideas are based on the wisdom of God. I'm not here to tell you what you should believe, but this much I do know: it takes faith and courage to succeed in this world, and you cannot do it without knowing who you are from a spiritual base.

FILL YOUR LIFE WITH HEROES

All of us need role models and mentors in our lives—people who inspire us and people who believe in us.

Role models are easy to find. You can read about them in books, or see them in movies, for instance. That's one of the great things about role models—people you don't even know can still be role models. Role models are people who set an example for you to follow as you build your life.

Mentors, on the other hand, are like private cheerleaders. They're the people in your everyday life who give you encouragement and support; sometimes they even help you find your path to success.

That's what happened to Judge Nelson A. Diaz. He was a tough, streetwise Puerto Rican kid who was headed for trouble until he met David Wilkinson, who had come to Harlem to work with neighborhood teenagers. Wilkinson helped Diaz turn his life around. "I could easily have ended up on the other side of the bench," Judge Diaz said. "He taught me how to have a sense of self-worth. I started working as hard as I could to get out of the ghetto. And I did."

Diaz was lucky: his mentor found him. But sometimes we have to look for our mentors. They're out there—in the churches and community centers, in your school, and maybe even in that store around the corner is an adult who would take an interest in you. Sometimes all you have to do is ask for the advice and help you need—because there are many, many good people in this world who care about kids and want them to have a good future.

You're about to meet some of them now.

There's no question that life is a challenge, but we are all capable of reaching down deep inside and overcoming our challenges. The heroes in this book prove that.

Their stories have made a difference in my life. I hope they will do the same for you.

—Rosey Grier

Rosey Grier's
All-American Heroes

David S. Bernstein

★ | *Success is, for me, the ability to say that I have*
      made a positive difference in the world.

At 26, David S. Bernstein has accrued a list of professional achievements a person twice his age would be proud to claim.

He's made headlines in two of the nation's most prestigious newspapers, *The Washington Post* and the *Boston Globe*. Television and radio shows regularly invite him to be a guest, and his work sparks debate on college campuses nationwide.

As founding editor of *Diversity and Division: A Critical Journal of Race and Culture,* Bernstein is staking out a place for himself in the national news community. *Diversity and Division* is sponsored by the Madison Center for Educational Affairs, a nonprofit, conservative think tank in Washington, D.C., where Bernstein works as a program officer.

Produced quarterly, the black-and-white, forty-page magazine is distributed free at more than forty college campuses. Editor Bernstein characterizes the journal as the only such magazine "written and produced entirely by people of the new generation—of the post—baby boom generation. Everyone who works on it is under thirty."

What that means, in simple terms, is that *Diversity and Division* approaches issues from the perspective of people who don't remember the 1960s and the racial strife that occurred as the civil rights movement came of age. *Diversity and Division* views racial issues from a perspective based on developments such as affirmative action—which Bernstein describes as "morally more problematic," because they're not as clearcut in terms of right and wrong as, say, segregation.

Diversity and Division challenges the status quo from all angles.

Among the topics covered in recent issues: "Planned Parenthood and the Perfect Race," an article that questions whether Americans, particularly racial minorities, should be concerned by the "dark legacy" of Planned Parenthood's founder, Margaret Sanger; "The Role of Black Churches," a feature that explores the history and declining influence of Christian churches in the black community; and a piece that examines why "rap group Public Enemy is neither funny nor harmless."

When *Diversity and Division* was launched in September 1991, Bernstein was 24—a tender age, by most accounts, to take a stand as a social critic. But the bespectacled, comfortably buttoned-up Bernstein seems to have been born to this role.

"From the time I was young, I was determined to do something 'special' with my life," he said. "When I was about 13 or 14 years old, I once told a group of adults that I was sure I would be famous someday. I didn't know what I would be doing, or how it would occur, but I truly believed that I would accomplish something of worth during my lifetime."

What inspires such ambition?

Much of the credit, Bernstein said, goes to his parents, who encouraged him and "always reinforced in me the notion that I could do whatever I set out to do." Equally important, they instilled in him a spirit of social responsibility, "the belief that we are all here to fulfill some higher plan—that who I am, and what I am doing, is not an accident but has some meaning and purpose."

A self-proclaimed conservative, Bernstein has distinguished himself as a critical thinker who's not afraid to confront complex social and political issues, or the racial stereotypes that come from being the son of a mother who is black and a father who is Jewish.

"I remember the first time I told my father I was becoming a conservative," Bernstein recalled. "I think I was about 15, 16 years old. And he was very confused about that."

That episode was an initiation for the many times since that Bernstein has been called upon to explain, even justify, his beliefs and the apparent abandonment of his heritage.

"There was a time when being conservative was really just equated with being racist," he said, "and there are a lot of people who want to make you continue to believe that myth."

David S. Bernstein

Up until the day of their son's pronouncement, the Bernsteins—like many people who consider themselves progressive and open-minded about race issues—characterized themselves as liberals. Yet they espoused values—respect your elders, respect your family, respect traditions—that would be considered conservative. "They never thought of themselves as conservative, just because being conservative was always bad," Bernstein said.

Though his parents were not "overtly political," he said, they created a family environment where discussion of social and political issues was common fare at the dinner table.

Bernstein can trace his political awakening to one other key influence: Jimmy Carter.

In 1980, when he was an eighth grader at Georgetown Day School, his class participated in a mock presidential election that opened his eyes to "the way the country was going," Bernstein recalled.

"You don't really know the issues behind it when you're 13, but you see that you're waiting in line to buy gas, you see that there's these hostages over there, been there for a year, can't seem to get them out, you try to get them out and you fail. And everyone just seemed generally blah and unhappy. That kind of turned me off from Jimmy Carter."

Despite conventional wisdom that black people should vote Democratic, Bernstein decided: "I like this Reagan guy. He sounds like he knows what he's doing. He wants to do everything opposite of Carter, which can't be bad."

Bernstein's been hooked on politics ever since. At the University of Maryland, he majored in government and politics, and became president of the campus's College Republicans. In 1988, he worked for the senatorial campaign of Alan Keyes, a black Republican, and the presidential campaign of Senator Bob Dole.

Then in 1990, Bernstein hit the campaign trail himself, as a Republican nominee for a seat in Maryland's General Assembly. By his account, he "did poorly—but had a lot of fun doing it." Undaunted, he successfully bid for a four-year term on the Republican Central Committee for Prince George's County.

That same year, he founded the Student Forum, a national organization of minority student leaders and young professionals dedicated to fostering open discussion of issues among young people. By 1992, the Student Forum numbered more than one hundred members.

Bernstein is also an accomplished author. He's been published in *The Baltimore Sun* as well as dozens of collegiate newspapers. His own publication, *Diversity and Division,* grew out of his involvement with other young black conservatives, in particular, at a 1989 Republican National Committee gathering of black collegians.

Bernstein and his fellow conservatives realized the need for a forum to exchange ideas representing diverse political viewpoints. "On college campuses, in the Black Student Union, there was a real lack of discussion on the issues, as only one political ideology was promoted," Bernstein said. "If you didn't have that perspective, you were automatically excluded."

Or worse. Speaking before the 1992 World Jewish Congress in Brussels, Bernstein recalled his experiences at the University of Maryland with tense race relations, particularly between radical black collegians and Jewish students.

"Five years of ongoing political battles with my fellow students, many of whom viewed me as a 'traitor to the race,' took a toll on me and on many other students I knew," Bernstein said.

"As a black, a Jew, a conservative, and a Zionist, I was *persona non grata* in the eyes of the radical black student organizations on campus. But what made me and a few others hated was that we refused to be intimidated by their icy stares, their thinly veiled threats printed in the college newspaper, or their revolutionary rhetoric aimed at cowing those who disagreed with their neo-Marxist, racist agenda."

Based on such experiences, Bernstein said, "Jewish student leaders and conservative activists, a small, often overlapping group with which I was involved, formed the only opposition to the Black Student Union's increasingly contentious manner of exercising its right to free expression.

"We protested, we put out leaflets, we held press conferences, all condemning the message advanced by the Black Student Union."

One thing led to another, as Bernstein's network explored ways to get their ideas heard. After seeking the advice of conservative scholar Leslie Lenkowsky, Bernstein was invited to set up an office at the Madison Center in June 1990. Little more than a year later, he was launching the longed-for literary mouthpiece.

"In America, millions of individuals from diverse racial and ethnic backgrounds have been molded into citizens by their adherence to common values," Bernstein wrote in his statement of purpose for the inaugural issue of *Diversity and Division*. "But a contrary concept—that America is not a society of citizens but a collection of races struggling for power—threatens the foundations of American democracy and has poisoned our public discourse about race, making it the most talked about but least understood subject in the nation."

Some of the same could be said of *Diversity and Division.*

When a University of Illinois political science professor cited *Diversity and Division,* "with its glossy cover and its wide distribution," as an example of the Right buying support for conservative ideas, Bernstein took the criticism in stride. Interviewed by the campus newspaper, he maintained that it was an insult to students' intelligence for the professor to suggest their support could be bought with slick packaging. But, Bernstein said, "If he feels that we're buying ideas with elaborate arguments, brilliant writing, and sound philosophy, then we'd plead guilty."

That kind of critical self-examination plus his ability to communicate, often eloquently, have been key to Bernstein's success. "I feel lucky and blessed because so few people my age have had the opportunities that I have to influence the larger world," he said.

At the same time, there is one thing about his life Bernstein would change: "I would get more out of my education at all levels. Often I coasted through school, including college, just to be able to get out and say I had a degree. While my life experiences outside of school have been extremely valuable in molding my character, I regret the wasted opportunity."

But the regret is balanced with optimism for the opportunities that await him. "I still have so much to learn, and hopefully, a lot more to contribute in my lifetime."

That outlook will undoubtedly guide Bernstein's career choices. "Starting a business and making a few dollars has never interested me, because I always want to say, 'How can I affect the larger world by selling shoes?' " he said.

"Success is, for me, the ability to say that I have made a positive difference in the world—that I have stood for ideas and ideals that are important to a free society, that I have done my best to advance and adhere to those values, and that my contribution will, in some way, have a lasting legacy on our society."

Already, Bernstein's work is turning heads: *The Washington Post,* in an article titled "New Kids on the Soapbox," characterized him as a fresh-faced but serious "twentysomething social critic." Bernstein doesn't shy away from the scrutiny that goes along with being in the spotlight. He is determined to live life on his own terms, and encourages other young people to do the same.

"Believe in yourself, that you, as a unique person, are meant to accomplish something positive in your lifetime. But don't measure success by other people's standards — material possessions are nothing compared with the spiritual fulfillment that comes from meeting your personal goals.

"Achievement through hard work is the only real success. You can never feel good about yourself if you haven't accomplished something that you can be proud of."

Tony Brown

★ *I learned early in life that all I was going to have was what I was willing to work for—I was taught that if you work hard, study hard and you are honest, whatever you want in life you'll have— within reason.*

Divide Tony Brown's views on race and economics into colors and you'd have three dominant hues—white, black, and green.

Whites, he argues, be it out of self-interest or racism, simply aren't going to give up their standard of living to help blacks. Most blacks, he has stated unabashedly, worship whites too much. Blacks have to learn to love themselves. Green—the color of money and power—represents true freedom: blacks should use their money to help blacks, and free themselves from the shackles of poverty, he believes.

Provocative thoughts from a provocative man. But then Brown's been raising eyebrows and turning heads for more than three decades while defining his niche in American media as an outspoken journalist who lives by a motto of self-help.

A man of action and accomplishment in many arenas, Brown preaches economic empowerment for blacks, arguing that government-run social programs alone can't cure poverty. His independent views have often set him at odds with other black leaders. For example, in 1991, Brown publicly announced that he was joining the Republican Party, a political affiliation that strikes most blacks as traitorous. One newspaper columnist said Brown had dropped a bombshell on his fans.

In typical fashion, Brown fought back. Attacking his critics in a column he wrote for *The Wall Street Journal,* Brown said: "Some black leaders foster a totalitarian environment in which any independent-thinking black who breaks lock-step with their often self-serving Democratic world-view is severely condemned, and even ostracized."

The Republican Party is the party of free enterprise, and poverty is the primary problem facing blacks, Brown said. "Blacks need economic solutions. And self-help is a time-tested economic solution."

Brown's beliefs are rooted in firsthand experience. He was born into poverty in 1933 in Charleston, West Virginia. Several brothers and sisters lived with relatives and neighbors because his parents couldn't afford to feed them. He attended segregated schools.

"I learned early in life that all I was going to have was what I was willing to work for," he said. "I was born in the middle of the Depression. In the black community, we had one black doctor, one black dentist, one black photographer, maybe two black lawyers. Schoolteachers and the postman basically rounded out the black middle class. No one had the stigma of poverty because no one had that much. I was taught that God would take care of you. I was taught that if you work hard, study hard and you are honest, whatever you want in life you'll have—within reason."

Brown made it out of West Virginia, after graduating from Garnet High School. He worked his way through college at Wayne State University in Detroit, Michigan, earning a bachelor's degree in sociology and then a master's degree in psychiatric social work.

But instead of becoming a social worker, Brown decided to pursue journalism, beginning his career as a critic. He went to the town's black newspaper, *The Detroit Courier,* and asked the editor if he could write a drama column. The editor replied, "We don't have any money, but if you want to come here and write, we'll teach you."

Brown accepted the offer. And within five years, he was regularly writing news and feature stories for the paper. About that same time, he also became involved in the civil rights movement. Brown's activism led him in a new journalistic direction—television broadcasting.

His career really took off in the late sixties after he discovered the Communications Act of 1934, federal legislation that said blacks had a right to have access to television air time. This prompted Brown, who was then president of the National Association of Black Media

Tony Brown

Producers, to file a lawsuit against radio and television stations—including the public TV station he was working at—to force them to hire blacks and to have black programming.

About a year later, in 1970, WNET-TV hired Brown as executive producer of *Black Journal,* the only national black TV show on the air at the time. Produced since 1968, the Emmy Award–winning show was renamed *Tony Brown's Journal* in 1977; the series is still aired on public television today.

The show proved to be a boon for Brown's career. The year after he launched it, he was asked by Howard University, a leading black college, to become the founding dean of the university's new School of Communications in Washington, D.C.

That marked the beginning of Brown's influence on education. Concerned with the shortage of blacks in the communications industry, he initiated an annual Careers Conference at Howard, which has been highly successful. He also founded the annual Black College Day in 1980; Congress has since officially designated the last Monday in September for this national observance. Brown also has spearheaded a movement to preserve black colleges through his work as the honorary chairperson of the National Organization of Black College Alumni, Inc.

During his media career, Brown also has ventured into films. He financed, wrote, directed, and distributed a $2 million movie called *The White Girl*—which is the street name for cocaine. The film deals with the issue of drugs and the self-hatred Brown perceives as prevalent in the black community. And he's produced a collection of documentaries called *The Library of Black History*, which he markets on videotape.

Always primed for a new opportunity, Brown routinely has a long list of projects in the works. He writes a syndicated column that appears in 150 black newspapers, publishes a quarterly magazine, and, most recently, signed on as a commentator for "All Things Considered," a show on the National Public Radio Network that reaches six million listeners.

He's also been working on his first book, entitled *No White Lies, No Black Lies—Only The Truth!* The book is scheduled for publication in 1993.

Brown's achieved status as a specialist on urban policies, cultural diversity, and economic development. At the height of the rioting following the Rodney King verdict in Los Angeles, he was one of twelve blacks invited to the White House to offer advice to President Bush.

As a man who truly lives by his words, Brown has proven to be an innovative entrepreneur. In 1991, he founded the Buy Freedom Network to promote economic self-empowerment among blacks. Through the network, blacks can dial a 900 number to find black-

or white-owned companies that offer the kinds of services they're seeking. Companies that participate in the network set aside some profits to fund job training and other programs designed to help minorities. Profits from the 900 number are used to support the Self Employment Enterprise Fund, a nonprofit group that guarantees loans for minority entrepreneurs who otherwise might not get them. Brown expects the network to foster some fifty thousand new jobs by the mid-1990s.

The self-help theme of the Buy Freedom Network is classic Brown. "Spending with black businesses will produce jobs within the black community and help stabilize conditions within the black community as a whole," he said.

"Blacks earn more than $300 billion a year. No matter how many programs blacks get to bring them into full employment, unless blacks retain a larger percentage of their money in their own communities and stimulate businesses to create jobs, then blacks will never catch up with whites."

Brown believes that freedom for blacks can only come from their ability to control their own economic destiny.

"Blacks place a fundamental overemphasis on the potential of white people and racism, and an underemphasis on the use of culture and group unity to defeat racism and achieve quality. The race problem will never be resolved so long as the black movement insists that white people give up a percentage of their standard of living," he said.

"If we continue to do that, whites will always oppose us—not necessarily out of racism, but out of self-interest. The bottom line is that the color of freedom is green."

Brown admits that his views are difficult for many blacks to accept. But he believes in his right to speak his mind and make his views heard, regardless of whom he might offend.

"If I were white, I wouldn't be unusual," he said of his tough stance on self-empowered economics. "I'm black and that makes me very unusual. I am not afraid of white people. I believe most black people are scared of white people. I don't think there is anything to fear. They are no better than I am. Black people for the most part worship whites too much. We have to learn to love ourselves."

Even those who don't agree with Brown's determined stance can't argue with the impact of this man, who was dubbed "Television's Civil Rights Crusader" in a cover story by *Black Enterprise* magazine. The New York *Daily News* named Brown's television series one of the top ten shows of all time for presenting positive images of blacks. Not long after, in Hollywood, the National Association for the Advancement of Colored People honored the series with a 1991 Image Award in recognition of Brown's efforts to present positive images of African-Americans.

But that's only a sample of the ever-growing roster of awards and honorary doctoral degrees recognizing Brown's achievements in civil rights, education, and journalism.

His pioneering efforts in education and broadcasting earned him the annual Solomon Carter Fuller Award from the American Psychiatric Association. Similarly, he's been cited at the Black Emmy Awards for distinguished achievement in the television industry. And Harvard University, as well as the American University of Paris, honored him during a special three-day celebration commemorating his twenty years on television.

Ever dedicated to fulfilling his motto of self-help, the controversial Brown's call to action is clear: "No white lies, no black lies—only the truth."

Roscoe Bunn

Be proud of who you are and never give up dreaming. Pursue those things in life that will make you a better person for life, not just for the moment. Get high on yourself.

Roscoe Bunn's life resembles an intricate patchwork quilt—rich in its diversity but ultimately a wholly connected image.

A smart youngster, he skipped a grade in school and ended up a college freshman at age 16. He almost decided to become a Catholic priest but was turned off by racist church attitudes. He rebelled in college and dropped out to pursue his love affair with car racing. Then he was drafted and found himself in the jungles of Vietnam. Back home after a two-year stint in the army, he worked two jobs to put himself and his wife through college. Today, he is a high-level sales executive for Avon Products, one of the world's largest companies.

Like a patchwork quilt, those varied experiences have common threads running through them. Dominant is his father, George Washington Bunn, a strong-willed man who was determined his bright, athletic son would make something of his life.

Bunn's father adhered to a powerful work ethic, never missing a day at his own job for thirty-three years. Proud of his black and American Indian heritage, he put his family first and taught his children that they could accomplish whatever they set their minds to.

This instilled in Bunn a desire to excel—at first, to please his father, but later in life, to satisfy himself that he could be an accomplished, professional black man and an upstanding human being who would make a difference in society.

"I always felt that I wasn't born with natural talent," Bunn said,

14

"and that if I aspired to be someone, I'd have to work hard. My dad was a proud man. He always used to say, 'If I wanted to be a success in the world, I would have to be better than any white or black male I competed with.'"

Whatever self-doubt he may have felt, Bunn exhibited a lot of natural talent from a very early age. Growing up in Chicago, he was an outstanding student all around. Skilled as an athlete, he experienced many victorious moments on the court and field, whether the sport was basketball, baseball, football, or track. In high school, he won several statewide athletic contests.

Bunn's academic and athletic achievements were inspired and supported by his dad, a strong disciplinarian and a devout believer in the power of a good education. He repeatedly told his son, "You have a home as long as you go to school."

Bunn remembers his folks as "the kind of parents that went to PTA meetings and participated in things. My father was at the beck and call of my teachers who had a performance or discipline issue with me."

To ensure his son received the best possible education, Bunn's father enrolled him in a Catholic grade school and high school in suburban Chicago. Bunn said that his father, like many blacks at the time, felt Catholic schools offered a better education than public schools and instilled greater discipline in children.

It was in grade school that Bunn considered devoting his life to religion and becoming a priest. But in high school, he had a change of heart after encountering racism and prejudice among school and church officials.

It was a disturbing discovery: "I really hadn't sensed any prejudice," Bunn recalled, "until my freshman and sophomore years in an all-boys school.

"This was the 1960s, so I tried to get them to support the civil rights movement and found them reluctant to participate. I was one of only five blacks in the entire school system and I experienced prejudice. I really couldn't understand how religion drew racist boundaries."

The experience was so bitter for Bunn he not only rejected the priesthood, but also convinced his father to let him transfer to a public high school.

15

Bunn graduated at age 15, entering Southern Illinois University just before his sixteenth birthday. Because he was so young, he was required to have adult supervision at the college. "We had adults who were like dorm parents," he said. "The guy I had was a retired soldier."

Adults strongly influenced Bunn. Because he was always younger than the people he attended school with, Bunn constantly had adults guiding him and setting boundaries. Often it was tough to balance the peer pressure he felt to be like the older kids with the pressure his parents exerted to make him abide by rules such as curfews.

"I had the exposure to do things, but not the opportunity," Bunn said. "I was involved with kids much older, but my parents treated me like the age I was."

The tension between Bunn's home life and school life increased in college, sparking intense disagreements with his parents. "All along I was aspiring to do the things that other kids were doing," Bunn said. "But I had a curfew and couldn't go to parties."

Bunn turned to his love of racing. Although his father wanted him to get a degree in business, a natural inclination and talent for working with cars had drawn Bunn to study mechanical engineering and race cars while in college. Wanting to be more independent, he finally decided to leave school and pursue his racing dreams. After dropping out, he began working at an auto parts store and service station. In his spare time, he started building his own race car.

Bunn's new lifestyle did not sit well with his father, who felt he was throwing away his education and failing to live up to his potential. Refusing to let that happen, the elder Bunn decided that, at the very least, his son was going to get a better job. Through a neighbor, he arranged an interview at Nabisco for his son.

Recalling the episode, Bunn said he went to the interview "somewhat under duress." Just the same, he got the job. Soon after, he also got drafted.

Once in the army, Bunn found himself eager to fight in the Vietnam War. Two of his close friends had been killed in combat within three months of being sent to Vietnam. "If anything, I felt a vengeance to go over there and even the score for the loss of those friends," he said.

Roscoe Bunn

In the army, just as in school, Bunn excelled. He volunteered for the Special Forces and became a Green Beret. He was in and out of active combat for the next fourteen months, and the things he was exposed to there would change his outlook—for life.

"To go to Vietnam and literally see people blown apart and maimed, to even have your first exposure to another country be that violent, was really an experience," Bunn said. "I found myself among the dying and those who wished they were dead."

His combat experience was so profound that Bunn, who had grown up hunting with his father, didn't pick up a gun for more than twenty years after leaving the army. He only started hunting seriously again a couple of years ago.

Though Bunn managed to return from Vietnam in one piece physically, he was a changed man inside. No longer feeling the youthful rebellion that had caused him to quit college, Bunn left the army determined to do what his father had always dreamed for him.

17

He was ready to get an education and make something of his life.

"Vietnam was the maturing point for me," Bunn said. "I had a number of close shaves where I was just lucky—sometimes it was just being a step out of the way. Fortunately, I made it back from Vietnam and I had a new attitude. When I came home, I wanted to do things right."

Bunn had married just before going to Vietnam. When he returned, he went to work again for Nabisco and enrolled in school. His wife also was in school. To support them, Bunn supplemented his Nabisco salary by also working at construction jobs. He completed his bachelor's degree and started pursuing a master's degree in business.

Just as in his early life, Bunn was drawn to people more experienced than he. Two veteran employees at Nabisco—a union president and a foreman—became his mentors. One black and the other white, the two men showed Bunn how to forge working relationships and how to get people with different personalities and backgrounds to cooperate.

"They reinforced the values that my father always taught me," Bunn said. "I always got coaching and feedback from them. It gave me a real balance. I got a lot of good vibes from a lot of good people."

While working toward his master's degree, Bunn was recruited by Avon. He left Nabisco to join the beauty products and direct sales company in 1977.

Bunn said he felt he "had arrived" when he was hired by Avon. Here he was—a black man who once thought of being a priest, a rebellious teenager who loved cars more than school, a highly trained soldier who had survived Vietnam—working as a supervisor in mainstream corporate America. His father's words echoed again—work hard, get an education, succeed. The dream was coming true.

Now when Bunn thinks back on the path he has traveled, his reaction is "Only in America."

Despite his enthusiasm and pride at being asked to join Avon, Bunn said the adjustment was anything but easy. "When I came to Avon I had a big Afro and was starting to grow a beard. I wore turquoise Indian jewelry," he said. "I came to Avon with a certain bit of pride and a little bit of arrogance."

Bunn's pride soon got in the way of promotions. His appearance made him stand out; his arrogance made others uncomfortable. Although he was continually given more responsibilities, Bunn began to realize that his career wasn't advancing. As had been his habit at other critical points in his life, Bunn turned to a mentor for advice and guidance. This time, it was a female manager who was willing to help him understand the situation and show him what it took to get ahead in a corporation.

"After some counsel from her, I quit trying to be 'blacker,' " Bunn said. "I realized who my friends were, and I started to trust them more and challenge myself to be an even greater contributor and participant."

Promotions followed Bunn's change in attitude. Today he is a sales executive for Avon's mid America region.

Equally important, Bunn makes it his business to be a role model and mentor for others, readily offering the kind of support that helped him survive the challenging episodes in his life. When Bunn meets young blacks just starting out in the work world, he passes along much of the same advice his supervisor gave to him. And because of the important role his father played in his life, Bunn is quick to help single mothers struggling to raise their children. It's not unusual, for example, for him to include a co-worker's son on weekend outings with his own family.

Bunn appreciates how easily his life could have turned out for the worse — if he hadn't had role models, if he hadn't held on to his own dreams, and if his parents hadn't instilled in him a strong desire to succeed.

He's the first to admit he made some bad choices along the way, and he has empathy for others trying to rebound from wrong turns or recover from events beyond their control. His teenage rebelliousness could have gotten out of hand and gone beyond the petty crimes he committed. He could have easily died in Vietnam. If not for his father, he might never have returned to college. If not for his first manager at Avon, he might not have survived at the company.

Bunn also knows what it is to overcome personal tragedy. His father died suddenly of a stroke one day as Bunn was driving to see him. Soon after, he lost his mother, which, in a different way, was an equally crushing blow. "She was the love and emotional support of my life," he said.

And he knows the pain of losing a child. One of his sons died at age 9 after mysteriously suffering a heart attack while running laps at football practice. Doctors later determined that the boy had a congenital heart problem the family hadn't known about. Bunn and his wife coped in part with their loss by adopting a child.

What's important about such experiences, Bunn said, is to learn from them and incorporate the lessons into your life. Two lessons Bunn has personally learned: value life and have self-respect. Whether facing a personal tragedy or simply surviving the effects of a bad decision, the goal should always be to set a better course for your life, he said.

Bunn offers this counsel to young people:

"Be proud of who you are and never give up dreaming. Pursue those things in life that will make you a better person for life, not just for the moment.

"Get high on yourself."

Ben Nighthorse Campbell

> *What the hell do you want in Washington, a fish?*
> *I can't imagine having some kind of vanilla*
> *milquetoast back there that won't fight. But then*
> *again, when people get in my face too much, I've*
> *been known to tell them off. I don't think you*
> *have to be a public doormat.*

Want the inside scoop about what's going on in Congress? Need a priccy, custom-made, native American gold bracelet encrusted with diamonds, opals, and turquoise? How about some advice on cattle rustling or horse breeding? Or maybe a few martial arts tips?

Then the man to turn to is Ben Nighthorse Campbell—rising political star, jewelry designer, rancher, judo master, and above all, free spirit.

Hardly your average guy, Campbell leads at least two very different and separate lives: that of the politician and that of the artist. A member of the Cheyenne tribe, Campbell became in the 1980s the first—and only—native American to serve in the U.S. Congress in years. What's more, in November 1992 Campbell made history, becoming the first full native American elected to the U.S. Senate in many years, breaking political ground for native Americans coast to coast. (In 1908, Robert L. Owen, who was ⅛th Cherokee, had won a senate seat from Oklahoma when it first entered the Union, and Senator Charles Curtis from Kansas, who later served as Herbert Hoover's vice-president, was part Kaw Indian.) Campbell defeated his Republican challenger by ten percentage points.

"Twenty years ago," said political consultant and pollster Floyd Ciruli, "it would have been a handicap to be a native American in Colorado. But between the native American rights movement and people like Ben Campbell, it is clearly a status position."

21

Indeed, despite — or perhaps, because of — his controversial political views and his offbeat lifestyle, Campbell continually wins hearts and votes. He's climbed peaks in two different careers and successfully straddles them both.

Campbell credits much of the success he enjoys now to a boyhood that schooled him in the art of survival. "Kids that come up tough tend to be tough," he said.

Campbell was born in 1933 in Auburn, California, to an alcoholic father and a Portuguese mother who spent twenty-two years in the hospital because she had tuberculosis. In fact, Campbell's parents met at the hospital while his father, Albert, was there trying to dry out from a drunken binge.

Those circumstances dictated the course of their family life. Young Campbell — whose middle name, Nighthorse, was given to him by the elders of the Northern Cheyenne tribe — spent much of his childhood in orphanages, in foster homes, and on city streets.

Campbell's chaotic upbringing had predictable consequences: "I was a bad kid. I was in a lot of trouble."

A high school dropout, he began turning his life around when he took a job picking fruit. Working alongside the children of Japanese immigrants, he was inspired to learn — and grew to love — judo. He trained hard and developed the skills and self-confidence to win the gold medal in the 1963 Pan-American games, and to become captain and gold medalist of the 1964 Olympic judo team at the Tokyo competitions.

His life as a young adult took many twists and turns. He joined the U.S. Air Force, and went on to earn a high school equivalency diploma. Then he put himself through San Jose University by working as a truck driver. He even worked nights as a police officer before heading back to Tokyo to study at Meiji University.

He married, and he and his wife, Linda, had two children. The family settled on a ranch among the Ute tribe in Ignacio, Colorado. There Campbell spent his days tending to the chores and making jewelry. Accustomed to shoveling cow manure in the barn, he never imagined himself hotly debating politics in Washington, D.C.

But one day in 1982, he happened to attend a local political meeting, and in an unexpected turn of events found himself a candidate in the race for Colorado's House of Representatives. It seemed no one from the district was willing to challenge the popular Republican opponent. So for reasons even he can't quite explain—he had no previous political experience or even political ambitions—Campbell agreed to take a shot at the state seat.

"I had never been to a [political] meeting, had never done anything at all," he said. "I was a registered Democrat because my mom was."

By most standards, it was a questionable beginning to a noteworthy career. But Campbell won his first race. In 1986, after four years in the Colorado House of Representatives, he went national, winning a U.S. congressional seat in a landslide victory. Campbell captured 52 percent of the vote in his district, where native Americans make up only 1.4 percent of the population.

In his home state, it seemed Campbell could do no wrong. But when he showed up for his first day of work in Washington, it was a different story. Straight off he broke a long-standing rule and was forced to get special permission just to walk onto the floor of the House of Representatives. Sporting a brightly colored scarf with an intricate native American—style clasp that he'd made himself—not exactly the "dress-for-success" look—he had violated the dress code that requires congressmen to wear traditional neckties. (He got permission to wear his scarf from then-speaker Jim Wright.)

Undaunted, Campbell has continued to proudly show his colors wherever he goes. At several points during his political career he's grown his hair long and pulled it into a ponytail. A living testament to the notion that you can tell a lot about a man by the clothes he wears, Campbell practices politics the same way he dresses: any way he pleases.

"I don't follow the party line," he said. "I'm even in trouble sometimes with the leadership. I vote independently because that's the way I want to do it."

Although he's now a U.S. Senator—and part of an elite group of politicians—Campbell doesn't plan to change his unique political, or sartorial, style. After winning his senate seat, Campbell promised that he wouldn't become another "three-piece suiter."

His ideas often clamor for controversy. Campbell has long supported multiple uses for public lands—a position that at times offends environmentalists who hold the narrow view that public

Ben Nighthorse Campbell

lands should be restricted for parks and wildlife. Some of Campbell's best friends in Congress strongly disagree with his stand on that and many other issues.

"People on both ends of the political extremes get upset with me," he said, "but I don't think that most American people are on either end of the political extremes."

Long before he begins upsetting his colleagues each day, Campbell is living the other half of his full life. Rising at dawn, he makes jewelry in his Capitol Hill home.

Carefully handling the precious gems and metals that go into his designs, Campbell works in the shadow of his heritage. On the wall above him hangs a painting of Custer's Last Stand, the battle in which his great-grandfather Blackhorse fought. The painting also represents something that's high on Campbell's agenda: changing the traditional view of his country's history, a view that either depicts native Americans as the "bad guys" or ignores them altogether.

Campbell sponsored legislation to rename the Custer Battlefield National Monument, proposing to call it the Little Bighorn Battlefield National Monument. And he wanted a new memorial erected to the tribesmen who died there.

The legislation passed overwhelmingly, but during the debate one senator accused Campbell of "trying to rewrite history."

Campbell shot back, "History wasn't written correctly in the first place."

With that in mind, he knew he was opening himself to attack when he and a descendant of Christopher Columbus served as grand marshals of the Rose Parade in Pasadena, California. Angry native Americans harshly criticized Campbell for waving to cheering crowds alongside a Spanish aristocrat. They felt the parade's theme, "Voyage of Discovery," was insensitive to their heritage.

"I knew full well I would get some flak from some Indians," Campbell said. "It's almost a no-win situation.

"Unfortunately," he added, "some of the people criticizing do not recognize the difference between tokenism and symbolism. I think we can make a very strong statement for American Indians. If you want to drop out and just protest, you can't tell the story."

Another story the politician is determined to tell: the dangers of Fetal Alcohol Syndrome (FAS). Caused when a mother drinks alcohol during pregnancy, FAS leads to brain injury and other abnormalities in the child. FAS strikes one in ninety-nine native Americans at birth—compared with one in every six to seven hundred people in the general population.

When Campbell learned about the illness, he said, "The first thing I thought was, there but for the grace of God go I."

25

Dedicated to fighting for his people, Campbell sponsored a bill aimed at preventing and treating FAS among native Americans.

Despite the strides he's made as a politician, Campbell still considers himself a jewelry designer first. This Senator predicts he would "go nuts" if he were "just a twenty-four-hour-a-day politician."

"You need an outside hobby to take your mind away from political office."

Like his political career, Campbell's jewelry-designing venture was launched by chance circumstances.

He learned jewelry making as a boy. When he was 12, his father schooled him in the basics — shaping, hammering, and sawing. But young Campbell felt the jewelry he created "wasn't that good" because his father used to joke that his son was more hurt than help.

Lacking confidence in his jewelry designs, Campbell abandoned his workbench for many years.

Then one day, when he was working as a counselor to native American convicts, Campbell wandered into an art store to browse. There in the showcase was a glittering surprise: a display of jewelry he had made as a boy.

This time, with the help and encouragement of the shop's owner, Campbell returned to his art, winning first place among three thousand entries at a state fair competition and walking away with the top three prizes at another competition.

His long-lost hobby became his newfound career.

"The freedom you get from being an artist is what appealed to me," he explained. "You can move around, you have flexible hours, you can work when you want — and not when you don't want to."

Today, celebrities wear Campbell's jewelry. It's not unusual for him to receive special commissions, or get as much as $20,000 for a single piece. His work can be spotted in museums and galleries across the map.

Campbell's contemporary native American designs are born of the world he loves most: the outdoors. He works with gold, silver, and precious stones from several nations. Sometimes he places gems on the undersides of pieces, hiding them from view — and revealing his own softer side.

"In Indian art, you believe a piece of jewelry — as with pottery, carving, or sculpture—should be like nature," he explained. "Even the parts you don't see are beautiful.

"If you were to look at a mountain, all you would see is one side, and that's beautiful. But there's another part that's equally beautiful that you can't see."

Daisy Chin-Lor

★ | *Throughout my life, I have taken opportunities presented to me and strived to be the best I could be. My parents always told me that I could be whatever I wanted and supported me in everything I did . . . .*

From the time she was a child, Daisy Chin-Lor understood that she was expected to work hard, to set an example, to make something of herself. She had her family's unflagging support in whatever choice she made, in whatever she did, as long as she was trying to be the best person she could possibly be. For her family, the desire to excel was treated almost as a credo—push yourself and your dreams will come true.

Chin-Lor's parents were even willing to leave their homeland, China, to fulfill their dreams. They came to America in 1945, arriving in postwar New York in search of a better life for themselves, and most importantly, their children.

They were determined to live the American dream. And as they raised their family, they instilled in Chin-Lor and her sisters a belief that anything was possible if they believed in themselves and their own potential.

The children also were taught that they had a responsibility to set a positive example, to pioneer a "different path" for Asians in the United States, Chin-Lor recalled.

"I grew up in a predominantly white neighborhood, and our family represented Asians to our neighbors as well as what others might think of *all* Asians. Because of that, my parents instilled in my sisters and me the 'mission' to stand out among the crowd, to be the best and set an example for all Asians. Being really different created in me an urge to excel, to walk ahead and not look back, and to set an example for future generations."

Chin-Lor has more than succeeded at that mission. Today, she is a highly successful and respected business executive who has worked around the globe for one of the world's largest corporations, and she is widely regarded as a leader in the Asian-American community. *The Los Angeles Times* has described Chin-Lor as "a minority success story"; for her parents, she is their American dream come true.

In honor of her accomplishments, Chin-Lor was named Woman of the Year for 1992 by the Chinese-American Planning Council, the largest provider of social services for Asian-Americans in the United States.

Henry Tang, a planning council board member, said he nominated Chin-Lor for Woman of the Year because "she exemplifies a most positive role model for Chinese-Americans, particularly the professional working woman who must juggle not only work but family and career commitments."

Chin-Lor has been married for fifteen years to Rolland Lor, an entrepreneur who has his own trading company based in New York and Hong Kong. They have one son, eleven-year-old Jonathan.

When the Chinese-American Planning Council named Chin-Lor Woman of the Year, she was touched by the recognition. But most of all, she was surprised by the unexpected honor.

"Throughout my life, I have taken opportunities presented to me and strived to be the best I could be," she said. "My parents always told me that I could be whatever I wanted and supported me in everything I did, and I think I owe my achievements and this award to my family's love, support, and pioneer spirit."

Like most working women, Chin-Lor sometimes faces tough choices as she juggles the complex demands of a family and a successful business career. But she wouldn't have it any other way.

"For me, success is being able to balance my career, my family life, and my personal interests, and getting the most fulfillment and enjoyment possible out of each," she said.

Asked how she achieves that balance, Chin-Lor offered these insights:

"Find the right people and systems that will support your demanding lifestyle. Focus on time management, set clear priorities, and be realistic about what can be done.

Daisy Chin-Lor

"Don't be afraid to say 'no,' or ask for help. And be proud of making the choice to have both a career and a family."

Chin-Lor began her business career not long after graduating Phi Beta Kappa in 1975 from Hunter College in New York. Her first job was as a buyer for Sears & Roebuck Company, which, at the time, was the nation's No. 1 retail chain. She worked for Sears for five years, until the company relocated to Chicago.

Chin-Lor wanted to stay in New York to be close to her parents and two sisters, so she began a job search that led her to Avon Products Inc., the world's largest direct marketer of beauty and related products. She joined the company in 1979 as a product counselor in its New York–based jewelry marketing group.

As she has done throughout her life, Chin-Lor excelled at Avon. She quickly rose through the company's marketing ranks, being named group marketing manager for prestige fragrances within five years.

Chin-Lor then took what many people might have considered a risky career move—she left the fast-track marketing group to join human resources as Avon's director of multicultural planning. The move paid off by giving Chin-Lor broader business experience. Within two years, Avon offered her a major promotion: an international position as the company's area director in Europe.

That promotion presented a turning point in her life and a test of her desire to balance work and family. "Clearly, it was the right career move," Chin-Lor said, "but it also was a major sacrifice for my husband, who had to give up his job; for my son, who had to relocate and make new friends; and for my parents, who were going to miss me."

Ever supportive of her success, Chin-Lor's family willingly made the sacrifices required for her to accept the promotion abroad. The move was a good one: after two years in Europe, Chin-Lor was sent to Hong Kong as regional director for Avon's Pacific markets. Then, in 1991, she was promoted again, this time to a highly visible post in a very competitive market—the kind of job that's coveted in most multinational corporations.

At the relatively young age of 38, Chin-Lor became president of Avon's subsidiary in Taiwan, one of the company's fastest-growing and most profitable businesses. As president of Avon Cosmetics Taiwan, Ltd., Chin-Lor runs a multimillion-dollar company with three hundred full-time employees and a sales force of forty thousand. She currently is one of only two women presidents among Avon's thirty-eight subsidiaries worldwide.

For Chin-Lor, being named president of a key Avon business wasn't just a tribute to her own hard work and determination, it was a tribute to the love and support her parents and family had given for years.

"My family has given me the strength to move ahead in uncertainty, the courage to take risks, and the determination to be the best," she said.

In a way, Chin-Lor's move to Taiwan brought her family's story full circle: her parents had left their native Asia to discover the American dream, and now Chin-Lor was back in Asia living it—the American-born daughter of Chinese immigrants, in charge of one of a major American corporation's most important businesses in the Pacific Rim.

As a first-generation Asian-American, Chin-Lor has helped pave the way for others. Still, she is low-key about whatever challenges she had to overcome to get where she is today. "I don't feel very different from other people I meet or friends or family," she said. "However, I have been lucky and had many opportunities, and I have a great network of friends and family to support me."

Remaining flexible has helped Chin-Lor excel and easily adjust to change and new environments. "All my positions at Avon have broadened my perspective," she said, "from marketing to area management to human resources. I feel I've been very fortunate—I was always open to new opportunities. If you hang your hat on a certain position, it might not be there when you're ready for it."

Chin-Lor's career also has benefited from some expert mentoring. Among the people she counts as key influences is Avon's senior officer in human resources, Marcia Worthing.

"I worked for Marcia for a number of years, and she was always a very good guide and mentor," Chin-Lor said. "I think it is particularly important for women to have another woman as a role model. She encouraged me and gave me hope for the future."

Chin-Lor has done no less herself. Among the employees who belong to Avon's Asian Network, Chin-Lor's career climb is legendary. "We think very highly of Daisy," said Shirley Dong, who heads the network. "As a role model, she's phenomenal because she is that rare mix of someone who's successfully blended her Asian culture with the American corporate culture."

Chin-Lor's life is a reflection of her family's support and encouragement. Her successes echo with her parents' teachings, which she gladly shares for future generations:

"Believe in yourself. Have the courage of your convictions, know your strengths, and don't hesitate. Seek support systems that encourage, build, and guide you to where you want to go and achieve your goals. Don't be diverted by the cynics, public opinion, or 'what's right to do.'

"Basically, make a difference in the world—because everyone has the ability to do it."

Johnetta B. Cole

★ | *Now, if you want to know my secret love, it is to be able to serve as an example.*

"Sister President" is what Spelman students call Johnetta B. Cole, educator, anthropologist, author, and, since 1987, president of the oldest institution of higher learning for black women in America. Often walking across the college campus for exercise, the statuesque Cole is a striking, yet always approachable presence as she talks with students and faculty.

As Spelman's first black woman president in the college's 112-year history, Cole brings a mixture of feminism, humanism, and black pride to her role.

She believes that education is the "most consistent and obtainable means for the empowerment of black women." Her goal is to make the college a renowned center for scholarship by and about black women, as well as the premier institution for educating and nurturing black women leaders. She advocates a strong liberal arts curriculum, yet is determined to keep it relevant to a changing world.

Although Cole believes that educational opportunities should be diverse, she also is convinced that attending a black women's college can be an invaluable experience for an African-American woman.

"What a black women's school provides is a setting that does not belittle her, it affirms her," she said.

Born in Jacksonville, Florida, in 1936, Cole grew up surrounded by an affectionate middle-class family, a supportive black community, and the unforgettable pain of a segregated South. She attended all-black schools.

On her first day in first grade, the teacher—respectfully called "Mrs. Vance, Ma'am"—asked students to give their names. Cole mumbled when it was her turn. The next thing she knew, Mrs. Vance towered in front of her.

"Stand up, look me straight in the eye, and never again, as long as you live, mumble who you are," the teacher instructed. That early lesson in self-esteem and dignity has carried Cole a long way.

"My greatest influences were black women in education," said Cole. She includes her mother, who taught English and was the registrar at Edward Waters College.

Cole was lucky to have positive role models, among them her great-grandfather. He often told stories going back to 1901, when church members made it a habit to "pass the plate" every Sunday.

"Somebody would stand up and say that brother Jacob's sister is ailing, could we help?" Cole recalled. "Or, we're sad to announce that sister Martha's husband passed, could we help?"

Her great-grandfather and others began a burial society that evolved into the Afro-American Life Insurance Company. It was an important institution at the time, because no white company would insure a black person.

"We must do for ourselves," these men said. Years later, after studying anthropology, Cole realized that their powerful message and the decision to start their own insurance company had roots in the Su Su tradition of West Africa.

In West African society, in order for an entire community to benefit, each individual must contribute to a pool. When someone is in need, that person receives the whole lot.

As an anthropologist, Cole often thought about African influences in African-American life. Pride in her heritage was never undermined by people claiming that black people had left their culture in Africa. She knew that within her family, there had been tangible evidence that the African ways were still very much alive.

"I had appropriately pushy middle-class parents," Cole said— though she was quick to add that it isn't always clear what middle class means in black communities. But she did grow up with a mom and a dad who were both college graduates, in an intellectual household where books and music abounded. Her father worked with the Atlanta Life Insurance Company, and later, in his wife's family's insurance business.

One of her vivid childhood memories is of sitting on the knee of black leader Mary McLeod Bethune. People suggested then that Bethune was the woman Cole should grow up to be.

"I remember very well the story about Mary McLeod Bethune beginning a college for little colored girls," Cole said. "I cannot tell you how many times I heard that story."

Cole always knew she was going to college. At 15, she took an exam and was accepted as an early entrance student to Fisk, an all-black college. Fisk was a tremendous influence in her life, because it provided firsthand exposure to black intellectuals.

"I grew up in the segregated South," she said. "I grew up where the library was the colored branch. I grew up where, for many years of my life, our house faced a park that had a fabulous swimming pool, swings, grass, benches — but I could not go there because all of that was for white people."

But Cole didn't complete her education at Fisk. Her older sister was at Oberlin, and Cole, claiming to be a copycat, transferred to join her. "I left Fisk, I think, because I simply didn't quite understand what Fisk was about. I mean, I was a pretty young kid," she said.

Cole wanted to be a doctor, until she went to a class at Oberlin on cultural anthropology. It was taught by George Eaton Simpson, and to this day, Cole can describe in detail his tall lanky body as he stood before the class playing Jamaican revivalist cult music. Simulating hyperventilation, he explained between breaths that he was sharing an expression of African culture in the new world.

That's what anthropologists do, Cole said, recalling that her career conversion was passionate and immediate.

"I think that many an intellectual, many a professional, is literally turned on by a moment, an encounter in a classroom," Cole said. "It's what ought to make those of us who are teachers really humble."

But when Cole later described that moment to her grandfather, telling him she wanted to be an anthropologist, he simply laughed. The businessman in him was focused on money — and how she planned to make a living.

Cole cried until her mother explained that besides making money, it was important to find work she loved — or she'd be miserable. That lesson continues to guide her even now, as Spelman's president.

Johnetta Cole   Photo: courtesy of Spelman College

"Out of that, I gained respect for the fact that our education must help us find work, though we must also respect students' passions," she said. "If there's a young sister who wants to be a poet, then we have to help her be a poet. We're not going to spend four years convincing her to be a computer programmer."

After graduating from Oberlin, Cole continued her education, earning both a master's degree and a Ph.D. in anthropology from Northwestern. In 1960, she married Robert Cole, a fellow graduate student, and the white son of an Iowa farmer.

When the couple visited Cole's family in Jacksonville, some white people threatened to bomb the family insurance business.

The couple spent the first two years of their marriage in Liberia, where Cole engaged in fieldwork. They had three sons, before divorcing two decades later.

Cole's distinguished career has been punctuated by many notable accomplishments. In 1965, she was named Outstanding Faculty Member of the Year at Washington State, where she was assistant professor of anthropology. In 1979, she received a tenured position at the University of Massachusetts, where she played a critical role in developing their African-American studies program.

From 1983 to 1987, Cole was a full professor in anthropology at Hunter College of the City of New York. During that time, she was director of the Latin American and Caribbean Studies Program.

It was during that period, while on her first visit to Cuba, that she started thinking seriously about gender. In 1986, she published a landmark book, *All-American Women.* The book broke new ground in women's studies because of its sensitivity to the intersections of race, ethnicity, class, and gender.

"What is particularly striking about Spelman is the coming together of the issues of race and gender," said Cole. "In other words, Spelman calls for dealing with bigotry about femaleness and color."

Cole sees women as socializers in America. She believes they have a special responsibility to bring the American dream of equality into reality.

"Until the day comes when men take their rightful place as co-nurturers, it is women who are our children's first and principal teachers of values, attitudes, and behavior patterns," said Cole.

She feels that by socializing our children to respect diversity, by encouraging our schools to teach the full history of America's many peoples, and by making certain that we behave in concert with the needs of a pluralistic society, women can be the catalyst for enormous change in America.

"One of these days, somebody is going to have to figure out how to get rid of racism and sexism—and that's an intellectual's job," said Cole.

Somebody is going to have to solve the network of problems and be responsible for socializing and educating future generations. She believes it's imperative that African-American women be part of that process.

For her part, Cole has directed her energies toward writing a new book, *Conversations: Straight Talk with America's Sister President.* In one section of the book, Cole analyzes the twin problems facing African-American women—racism and sexism.

Scheduled to be released in early 1993, the book has been described by her publisher as an "exhortation, a call to arms, one that is expressed with great love, great affection, and enormous enthusiasm."

Cole has long held the belief that a good liberal arts education is a must because it gives students not only skills and information, but a sense of the world in relation to themselves. A black student isn't well educated if she knows world history and American history, but hasn't studied black history, Cole argues. And since that history didn't happen in a vacuum, whites who don't know it aren't well educated, either.

It's a shame that teaching, which once drew the brightest and most creative women, no longer attracts them, says Cole. While she's not calling for a return to sex-biased occupations, Cole does suggest that by moving into traditionally male-dominated fields, women have not considered another option: redefining teaching from a feminist perspective. Because it used to be an all-female profession, teaching is too often given secondary consideration by many of today's career women.

Despite the fact our country does not sufficiently value and foster teaching as an extraordinary experience, Cole encourages Spelman students to consider academic careers. If they don't, she sees problems ahead.

"Then the Harvards, the Hunters, the Yales, the Wisconsins, and the Spelmans will continue to say, where are the black faculties?"

Sister President's dream is that Spelman will become even stronger as a school that expresses the very best in intellectual life and community service. Cole dreams of making Spelman a place where students and faculty revel in ideas — but not sterile, scholastic ones.

"They've got to be ideas that address issues of inequality, ideas that address how a society indeed takes advantage — or exploits, if you will — the full capabilities of every member of our society," she said. "That's one of the things I want to be remembered for."

Bill Cosby

I envision a world where African-American children no longer say "May I?" They will self-assuredly say "I will," and know that their highest ambitions and goals are realistic and can be achieved.

On September 20, 1984, America tuned in to NBC to watch thirteen-year-old Theo Huxtable of *The Cosby Show* explain to his dad why he didn't need or want the pressure of getting good grades.

The elder Huxtable listened calmly, patiently, and sympathetically as Theo presented his case: good grades didn't matter, Theo reasoned, because after all, he only wanted to be a "regular person."

The TV camera zeroed in on Cliff Huxtable, who was regarding his son with thoughtful silence. Then, the man who would become America's No. 1 dad suddenly burst out, "That is *the most* ridiculous thing I've ever heard!"

With that, the audience exploded into laughter and Bill Cosby launched into a message dear to his heart: education is essential. The soliloquy was delivered in classic Cosby style by a man who never completed high school. And from that opening episode, Cosby's new show would change the course of television history.

In creating the series, Cosby believed that people were starving to see children show respect for parents and parents show respect for children. But would anyone actually watch? ABC and CBS executives didn't think so and turned down the series. Even Cosby had doubts.

"I was just hoping there would be enough viewers so that we could stay alive," he said.

Prime time airwaves B.C.—Before Cosby—were cluttered with often violent action-adventure shows, such as *Magnum P.I.,* and fantasy soap operas, such as *Dynasty,* that disguised greed as glamour.

It took a lot of channel changing to find a family-oriented sitcom. And what few could be found relied heavily on meaningless gags, outrageous situations, and stupid parents to salvage their sinking ratings.

But even after *The Cosby Show* began raking in more praise, more fans, and certainly more money than any other TV show ever, it still had critics.

The series, some people complained, wasn't "black enough." The Huxtables were too normal, too happy, too perfect, too well off. It was just another *Fantasy Island* in television land, but this time, the island happened to be in Brooklyn; there was no place on Cosby's block for the realities of black family life: racism, drugs, violence, poverty, and the struggles of single parents, critics argued.

Yet, for all the same reasons, the show won significant support. Coretta Scott King, widow of slain civil rights leader Martin Luther King, Jr., championed Cosby's colorblindness, saying his series was the first to let a black middle-class family be just that—a black middle-class family.

In a humorous way, each episode tackled the problems of everyday family life: how to break the news to five-year-old Rudy that her goldfish had died; coping with Vanessa's crush on a schoolmate; dealing with Denise's decision to drop out of college; confronting the issue of teenage sex; and, of course, staying on top of Theo's continuing bad grades.

But it was Phylicia Rashad, the actress who played Clair—the show's tough but tender wife, mother, and lawyer—who finally shut up the "it's-not-black-or-real-enough" critics. Her response, coolly delivered in no-nonsense Clair fashion, was that these folks might just "have a problem in that they think of themselves as the only human beings on the planet. And when they see people who are not white in human circumstances, they feel we are not what we are supposed to be."

Or, as Cosby put it, "I was aiming to break a mold."

Breaking molds—daring to be different by standing up for one's personal, however unpopular, beliefs—not only made Cosby one of the most influential and respected men in television, it didn't hurt

Bill Cosby

his career or his bank account either. Cosby is considered one of the wealthiest people in the country; according to one business magazine, the actor is worth more than $300 million.

From the earliest days of his career, Cosby dared to break new ground. He was the first black to co-star in a TV drama. *I Spy,* which ran from 1965 to 1968, won Cosby his first Emmy Award for portraying secret agent Alexander Scott, a black man who was a part of white society and, at the same time, comfortable and proud of his heritage.

Cosby also set records in the field of comedy. His twenty-four albums have sold more copies than any other comedy album ever. Even now, he is in constant demand to entertain at the country's biggest and best night clubs.

But for all of his success, Cosby has suffered his share of setbacks, including two TV sitcoms that quickly vanished from the airwaves and two variety shows that both did disappearing acts after short screen lives. And his career as a movie star never amounted to much. In the seventies, he made four movies which earned reactions that were, at best, mixed—critically and commercially. Those movies: *Mickey and Boggs* and *Uptown Saturday Night,* made with Sidney Poitier as co-star and director of a cast that included Harry Belafonte, Flip Wilson, and Richard Pryor; and *Let's Do It Again* and *Mother, Jugs and Speed.*

But even when his star seemed to dim, Cosby's self-confidence and determination remained strong. "I'm very good," he once said.

Drawing upon his career in children's television, including his Saturday morning hit, *Fat Albert and the Cosby Kids,* his appearances on *Sesame Street* and *The Electric Company,* his work as an instructor in prisons, and his own life, Cosby compiled his experiences into a dissertation for the University of Massachusetts at Amherst.

In 1977, the college accepted his 242-page dissertation and awarded him a doctor of education degree. The gesture seemed to say that even top teachers supported Cosby's notion that good television can be good for kids.

Not bad for a two-time dropout—Cosby quit both high school and college.

It was back in his hometown of Philadelphia that young Cosby, a talented student and captain of his high school's track and football teams, was told that he would have to repeat the tenth grade. Despite considerable intelligence—he was assigned to a class of gifted students—Cosby's academic performance was poor. Rather than prolong his education at Germantown High School, Cosby dropped out.

For a brief while he contributed to the family income—which

sometimes had to be supplemented with public assistance—by shining shoes and delivering groceries. Then in 1956, he followed in his father's footsteps by joining the U.S. Navy.

That's when everything changed for the young man who typically had treated life like it was a big joke. (A sixth-grade teacher once wrote on his report card that he was "an alert boy who would rather clown than study.")

But the navy imposed its own brand of discipline on the quickwitted young man. "The navy made me get up at 3 A.M. and stand and watch the clothesline, with no clothes on the line at all," Cosby said. "When I found out how much I hated that, I had to reexamine what I could be."

Before navy life, he had earned a high score on an IQ test and was told he should be a doctor or lawyer. But, he said, "I was really afraid to do these things, because it meant work." Being in uniform gave Cosby a new attitude after he realized he was serving "under people I knew I was much brighter than.

"At the end of about three weeks," he recalled, "I went to the base commander and I thanked him for what the navy had done for me and told him that I was now ready to go college. So I changed from an underachiever to a point where I realized that I had to get out and earn it."

But it took a lot more than a simple "Thanks, but no thanks" to satisfy his military obligation. Cosby stayed in the navy for four years and learned to be a physical therapist, eventually working at Bethesda Naval Hospital in Maryland. He also managed to earn a high school equivalency diploma through correspondence courses.

With the help of a track and field scholarship, he enrolled at Philadelphia's Temple University, where he majored in physical education. Then a scout for the Green Bay Packers saw the burly six-footer play and suggested that he might succeed in a career as a professional football player.

A life in the limelight, complete with cheering fans, must have appealed to the then sophomore—but he wanted no part of bulky uniforms and broken bones. Instead, he headed for the stage. For five dollars a night he started tending bar and telling jokes at a local coffeehouse.

Soon after, he took a temporary leave of absence from school, boarded a bus to New York City, and entertained at the Gaslight Cafe, a Greenwich Village coffeehouse that gave the likes of other well-known comedians such as Woody Allen a break. Before long, his "temporary" leave became permanent; once again he quit school, forfeiting a college degree to pursue a career as a comedian.

It was around this time that he went on a blind date with Camille Hanks, a psychology student at Stedman College in Atlanta. Married in 1964, they, like the Huxtables, now have four daughters and one son: Erika, Erinn, Ennis, Ensa, and Evin. All the kids' names begin with "E" for "excellence," their dad explained.

But their son was a bit of an exception. At age 13, Ennis started bringing home bad grades. Cosby recalled, "I sat him down and said, 'We're going to talk, and I want you to say whatever is on your mind.' We talked until 4:30 in the morning. And he said he wanted to be regular people. He didn't want the pressure of studying."

Like father like son, and eventually, like Theo Huxtable. In fact, many of Cosby's ideas and greatest sitcom scenes are drawn from episodes in his personal life.

Over eight years, viewers watched Theo's learning struggles follow the same uphill, rocky road that Ennis's took. As it turned out, neither Ennis nor Theo was lazy or stupid. They were tested and found to have dyslexia, a learning disorder that makes reading especially difficult. In both real life and the series, the parents saw the diagnosis as cause for celebration. Dyslexia could, and would, be treated at a special school where both Ennis and Theo were taught skills to cope with the problem and turn their lives around for the better.

After the dyslexia show, Cosby said, viewers wrote letters that said, "Our child was tested and we changed our behavior toward the child. We stopped calling him lazy." The way Cosby sees it, "That was a giant thank you."

The public also has supported and lauded Cosby in other ways. They made his books, *Fatherhood, Childhood,* and others, best sellers. Top companies such as Kodak, General Foods, Ford Motors, and Texas Instruments awarded him high-paying contracts to pitch their products.

But, as with many of his career moves, the advertising work cost Cosby some fans. While he went on TV to praise Coca-Cola's "New

Coke," people seemed to prefer the "old" formula and lost faith in Cosby's believability. He also promoted E.F. Hutton, a money management firm that pleaded guilty to fraud. Other people said that he was just selling too many products.

Nothing, though, would deter him—nor would he deter others. Just the opposite. Calling *The Cosby Show* quits after eight smash seasons, the cast and crew threw a huge farewell party on their final night together. During the festivities, the star made a point of seeking out twenty-one-year-old Malcolm-Jamal Warner, the actor who had played Theo.

"Has anyone seen Malcolm?" Cosby asked staff member after staff member. "I want to give him something."

That something turned out to be a red-and-blue baton. And when the TV dad looked his college-graduate sitcom son straight in the eye and silently handed him the baton, the meaning of the symbolic gesture was clear: you have a responsibility to be true to yourself, to run your own race and be your own kind of winner, Cosby seemed to say.

Then America's No. 1 dad gave Theo a fatherly hug and drove off into a rainy New York City night.

Dinesh D'Souza

★ *Success is defined by one's ability to tell the difference between what's right and wrong, and to strive as best as humanly possible to do what's right. To me, success and goodness are synonymous.*

When seventeen-year-old Dinesh D'Souza left India and landed in America, he looked around and saw no surprises. The deserts and the mountains, the cities and the skyscrapers, the ghettos and the glamour all looked familiar. After all, he had spent many hot Bombay afternoons seeing America at the movies, as *Rocky, Butch Cassidy and the Sundance Kid, The Sting, Bonnie and Clyde,* and *National Lampoon's Animal House* flickered across the screen.

Yet surprises and unexpected turns are par for the course for D'Souza, a complexly adventuresome fellow who believes in keeping an open mind to all possibilities.

As a child in India, he never dreamed he would end up marrying and settling in the United States, working in the White House as a domestic policy analyst, creating a flurry of controversy with his ideas, or, for that matter, becoming known as a high-brow intellectual who also manages to be a down-to-earth guy.

But little that he or anyone else does happens by pure chance, D'Souza believes. "The thoughts in our minds are the rudders for the things we do," he said.

Thinking is what D'Souza does, mostly—and he gets paid for it. As an author and political activist, D'Souza makes his living pondering questions such as: "How do we create an educational system that has equal rules for everyone? How do we get rid of poverty without punishing the privileged? How do we give everyone a fair shake?"

Growing up in the world's largest democracy, D'Souza was inspired by "good books and good people," he said. "I had the benefit of a strong and cohesive family, and have also been fortunate to have good teachers. I had a happy childhood."

While he liked playing field hockey, cricket, badminton, and Indian games, he also studied English and Hindustani (the main language in India) at a tough, traditional Catholic Jesuit school. There he developed a fascination with Western and Eastern literature.

"Books give you a window into experiences that are often deeper than the ones we have in everyday life," he explained.

His parents were practical people, but young D'Souza dreamed of adventure and exploring new worlds. So when he wasn't playing sports, he dived into "wild and fantastic fairy tales and adventure stories."

His American adventure began in a small-town Arizona high school; with the help of funds from the Rotary Club, he participated in a one-year exchange program. Back then, he was uncertain about his career plans, his interests, his whole future.

So even when he made the decision to stay in America after high school graduation, D'Souza still faced a lot of tough questions and a dubious future. "It was quite difficult for me to figure out how I would make ends meet to stay in this country to study and work," he recalled. Short on money, he soon discovered "the process of applying to college was both a trying and a difficult one."

And, back in India, his family was having mixed feelings too.

"Believe it or not, my dad and mom felt that they would like to see more of me," he said with a gentle laugh. But they also realized that their son—whose first name means "God of the Sun"—would be exposed to opportunities in America that he would never have in India.

So in 1979, he headed off to New Hampshire to major in English at Dartmouth College. There, he soon began writing for the campus newspaper, working in the international students' association, joining an energy conservation committee, and eventually, helping to start the *Dartmouth Review,* a politically conservative magazine that became nationally notorious for attacking the college's administration and taking controversial stands on minority issues.

But in his defense, D'Souza is quick to mention that the college administration regarded him as a "moderating and constructive" influence on the magazine.

Motivated by what he describes as "an interest and an ability to explore the world of ideas, and attempt to relate it to the world of action," D'Souza's policy judgments and his writings—including four books and numerous newspaper articles—aim to "excavate the world of scholarship and relate it to practical questions of what should be done."

Among the issues D'Souza said he regularly grapples with: "How should we address the problems of poverty or crime or declining educational standards?"

He draws his inspiration from Socrates, the ancient Greek philosopher. "By all human standards," D'Souza said, "Socrates was a kind of disgrace. He was poor. He was ugly. He was virtually homeless. He was unemployed." But, D'Souza said, "he understood the virtue of friendship and of conversation."

By most people's standards, D'Souza has made a success of himself very young in life. At age 26, he was advising President Reagan on issues such as civil rights, constitutional questions, and AIDS. Before that, he was managing editor of the magazine *Policy Review,* and before that, editor of *Crisis Magazine,* a Catholic monthly publication of news and opinion.

But he is probably best known as the author of *Illiberal Education: The Politics of Race and Sex on Campus.* Published in 1991, the book rocketed D'Souza to literary stardom. More than three dozen publications, including the prestigious *The New York Times Book Review,* reviewed or wrote articles about his book.

"It is a brisk, hard-hitting, sometimes strident journalistic tour through the political land mines imbedded these days in higher education," *The Wall Street Journal* wrote.

Business Week, in its review, said, "Many universities don't want to talk about the issues raised by affirmative action, curriculum revisions, special studies, and other efforts to redress past social injustices. But a most unlikely self-appointed substitute has stepped forward to do so."

Business Week characterized D'Souza "as a sort of Indian William F. Buckley, Jr.," because of his Catholicism, Ivy League background, courtly manner, and mischievous wit.

Dinesh D'Souza

Indeed, one of the consequences of becoming a best-selling author was that suddenly D'Souza was much in demand to discuss his book. In a twenty-city media tour, he appeared on network talk shows and news programs such as *Face the Nation, This Week with David Brinkley, Good Morning America,* and *Nightline.*

He also won fans on college campuses; in a space of nine months, he gave more than sixty lectures, often speaking without notes, on the issues that prompted him to write *Illiberal Education.*

Though his ideas are weighty, D'Souza, ever the down-to-earth fellow, delivers them with an engaging ease. Here's how one reviewer described D'Souza's appearance at Centre College, a liberal arts school in Danville, Kentucky:

"At the podium Dinesh D'Souza looks disarmingly genuine—too young for subterfuge, and too friendly. He woos the crowd openly with an ingratiating joke: 'When I got to Centre College earlier today I asked one of the students whether the college has a reputation for being very activist, and I was told that, no—Centre is known for being a hotbed of rest.' He is rewarded with a big laugh."

Already at work on a second book that examines the issues of race relations and human rights from a global perspective, D'Souza, now 32, is decidedly matter of fact when he discusses his past successes—or his future.

He does not, he said, "think in terms of 'making it.' I don't think there is a threshold that separates those who have 'made it' from those who have not."

If anything, he defines making it "as the continuous striving for knowledge. The search is always motivated by the hope of finding something, but even when you think you've found it, you still have to be open to the possibility that you're mistaken. Maybe part of making it is the ability to sit back and ask yourself, 'Where is my life going?' and not to be enslaved by one's circumstances to such a degree that you can never even ask the question or alter the circumstances."

D'Souza, highly praised and sharply criticized, seems to appreciate the attention he garners—even when it's the negative kind. He's been confronted with claims that he's glib, but more biting and more common are the accusations that label him an enemy of multiculturalism because, while he clearly defends equal opportunity for minorities, he is also against affirmative action policies.

At the same time, the criticism bothers him: "All criticism *should* bother you in the sense that it does make you ask whether you are mistaken or misunderstood, and if so, why."

It's how a person reacts to his critics that counts, he said. "You might respond to criticism by admitting your mistake. You might respond to it by saying 'Look, maybe I didn't express myself well.' You might respond to it by saying 'I don't agree with you, but that doesn't make me a bad guy.' "

Even though D'Souza's life journey has taken him so far in such a short time, he thinks that kids "should not try to grow up too fast. We spend most of our time as adults, so one should not be in too much of a hurry."

And he offers these insights to young people. First, recognize and take advantage of the opportunities America offers. Equally important, he said, everyone should "make one good friend and read one good book that is going to change their lives."

D'Souza has jumped many hurdles and he has jumped them both far and high, thanks in part to influences that have guided his life. "A believing Catholic but a poorly practicing one," D'Souza said religious faith is vital to achievement. He also believes a supportive family and friends are "indispensable," as is "a belief in one's own potential for good."

Still, all three—faith, support, and self-confidence—can be taken too far, and beliefs alone cannot make you a good person. "Good deeds," he said, "are not the function of philosophy but of habits. You are honest not because you have reflected on the moral necessity of honesty, but because you have been *taught* to be honest and you are used to saying what happened and what didn't happen."

It took a great deal of reflection and twelve years of searching for answers before D'Souza decided to become an American citizen. Feeling suspended between the American and Indian cultures, he procrastinated. And while he procrastinated, he considered what being an American citizen meant, what America's founding principles stand for, and "what place American society makes for immigrants and outsiders."

Given all that, he wondered, was he really at home here?

"I ultimately concluded that I was," said D'Souza, who on October 15, 1990, took his oath of citizenship.

And while D'Souza the intellectual knows a lot about American literature, government, and history, D'Souza the adventurer has his eye on worlds he's yet to explore.

"I don't know enough about art and music," he said. "I'd like to know more about the blues, sculpture, and architecture." But most especially, he wants "to spend more time seeing the country in the way that it differs, and yet in the way that it's held together."

Nelson A. Diaz

★ | *Nothing is impossible — if you don't believe, you can't achieve.*

They were a mismatched pair: an illiterate Puerto Rican teenager schooled on the mean streets of New York's Harlem and a "hillbilly from western Pennsylvania" hoping to help. But as Nelson A. Diaz describes it, that well-intentioned hillbilly saved his life. Instead of roaming the streets, Diaz began hitting the books and eventually became the unimaginable for a fifteen-year-old ghetto kid — a prominent judge and respected community leader.

"I didn't have the love of my natural father," Diaz said. "I grew up without a sense of self-esteem. I was involved in gang activity. I hung tough on the street. I thought I was tough because I survived and I had friends that didn't survive."

From the time he was a small boy, Nelson's life was a troubled mess that held little hope for a brighter future. "I didn't speak English until I was 8," he said. "By the time I was 15, I was in the ninth grade and I was illiterate in two languages. My only aspiration was to play baseball." Then one day David Wilkinson, whom Diaz affectionately calls a Pennsylvania hillbilly, arrived on Harlem's streets to work with neighborhood teenagers. Life for Diaz would never be the same.

"If it wasn't for the love that hillbilly showed us," Diaz said, "I could have easily ended up on the other side of the bench. He taught me how to have a sense of self-worth. I started working as hard as I could to get out of the ghetto. And I did."

Diaz went from the ghetto to college, earning a bachelor's degree from St. John's University in 1969. He then went to Temple University, breaking barriers to become the first Hispanic in the school's history to earn a law degree. While attending the university, Diaz

55

became an outspoken leader—a stance he has taken throughout his career. Annoyed by the lack of minority students at the university, Diaz pressed administrators to recruit more blacks and Hispanics and was instrumental in founding student law associations for blacks and Hispanics.

After earning his law degree, Diaz stayed in Philadelphia instead of returning to his native New York. There, he broke another barrier, becoming the first Puerto Rican to be admitted to the bar in Pennsylvania. Continuing the pattern he established as a law student, Diaz also became a community leader and civil rights activist.

In 1975, Diaz was named the Philadelphia Jaycees' Outstanding Young Leader of the Year. He has been instrumental in the development of social and health services in Hispanic neighborhoods in the city. He also raised awareness in the legal community of the needs of Hispanics, advocating the use of bilingual legal documents and fighting to get Spanish-speaking police officers in Hispanic neighborhoods.

Throughout the seventies, Diaz continued to build his career and his credibility as a concerned civic leader. He worked in two Philadelphia law firms, served as a special assistant to Vice President Walter Mondale, and was the executive director of the Spanish Merchants Association of Philadelphia. He also worked as a public defender and associate counsel of the Temple Legal Aid Program. For almost three years, Diaz was even a columnist for *The Philadelphia Sunday and Evening Bulletin.*

In 1981, Diaz reached a milestone in his legal career and broke yet another ethnic barrier: he became the first Hispanic judge in Pennsylvania's history. Diaz was appointed a judge in the Court of Common Pleas in the first judicial district of Pennsylvania by the governor, then elected later that year to a full term. He still serves on the bench today.

Diaz is a self-proclaimed workaholic, arriving at his office each day by 7:15 A.M. and leaving late. After more than a decade on the bench, he has earned praise from fellow judges for the "intelligence and vigor" he brings to the courts.

"I come from a poor, minority background," Diaz said. "Coming from such a background, my work ethic is that I have to do things better than most in order to be accepted and respected. The harder you work, the more you make yourself indispensable."

Nelson Diaz

Because of his tireless involvement in the community, Diaz also is known throughout Philadelphia as an honest and fearless political reformer. That reputation put Diaz, at age 43, in the political spotlight: in 1991, he was appointed by the state's Supreme Court judges to clean up Philadelphia's bloated and inefficient court system.

Philadelphia's city courts were legendary as a repository of local political patronage jobs. As a result, the system was bogged down by inefficiency and burdened with a huge backlog of cases. Diaz attacked the problems immediately with characteristic zeal. In the eighteen months he served as administrative judge, Diaz slashed budgets by millions of dollars, improved the court system's efficiency, and instituted case flow procedures that reduced the backlog.

Besides earning praise from local and state officials and the legal community, Diaz's efforts were recognized by the Foundation for the Improvement of Justice. The foundation awarded Diaz $10,000 for changing the "business as usual" attitude of the court system.

Today, in addition to serving as a trial judge in Philadelphia, Diaz remains active in local youth programs and community development projects. His list of professional activities, extracurricular interests, and professional and civic honors fill almost four typed pages. Among his many honors and awards: honorary doctoral degrees from three universities; the St. John's University Medal of Honor (the highest award given to an alumnus); the National Puerto Rican Coalition Life Achievement Award; a prestigious Fulbright grant to work with the Ministry of Justice in Peru; and Citizen of the Year in 1992.

Diaz works hard to be the same kind of role model that David Wilkinson was to him. He has encouraged countless numbers of teenagers to pursue their education and fulfill their dreams.

"The breaking of the barrier is important," he said, "to prove that we can do it, and so that someone will follow in these footsteps and know that they can lead the court."

Besides his long list of professional and civic accomplishments, Diaz also has found immense personal satisfaction from religion. The same week in 1991 that he was appointed to reform the city court system, Diaz also was asked to head the Billy Graham Crusade in Philadelphia.

Through his work with Graham and the crusade, Diaz found God. Now he rises each morning at 5 A.M. to pray for two hours before going to work.

"I never realized God could be that important in your life. I just can't get enough," he said.

"Prayer is an unbelievable resource. I don't feel I'm indispensable anymore. Hey, if they want to get rid of me tomorrow, fine. I'll find something else to do. I don't have to prove myself to anybody but God."

The support of family and friends, faith in yourself, and spiritual beliefs are essential for anyone who wants to achieve their goals, Diaz said. A man of integrity who will judge his life a success if it "improves the status for future generations," Diaz offers these words of encouragement to young people: "Nothing is impossible if you believe and try, try again. If you don't believe, you can't achieve."

Renee Du Jean

I don't feel as if I've "made it." Because I believe that you don't *make it. One should always be in the* process *of making it. And when you think that you've made it, you've finished this life. There always has to be something out there to strive for so that you* continue *to stretch and reach — for fear that you'll sit back and do nothing.*

Like most children, Renee Du Jean loved sleep-overs. One morning, when she was 5 years old, she awoke to breakfast at her Aunt Bea's house, not far from her own home in Brooklyn, New York.

"I'm going out for a minute to buy a newspaper," her aunt said. "Is there anything in particular that you'd like to read?" she jokingly asked.

"The New York Times," the little girl replied.

That stopped Aunt Bea in her tracks. At that time — it was the 1940s — the nation's most respected paper, the paper with the motto "All the news that's fit to print," had no room for comics and barely fit in a few pictures. So what in the world would a five-year-old possibly want with *The Times?* Still, Aunt Bea dug into her purse for the three cents that the paper cost back then. She must have figured it couldn't hurt to indulge her niece.

"I spread this huge paper on the floor, so that I could read it," Du Jean recalled with a slight laugh. And read it she did, poring over news of politics, business, sports, theater, and everything in between.

Moments like that proved early on that Du Jean was going to be anything but average. She wasn't like most kids, and as an adult, she's built a reputation as a strong leader with innovative ideas and a determination to get the job done right.

"I had a head start in learning in that I was always a reader," said Du Jean, who heads the Black Executive Exchange Program, better known as BEEP. Through a variety of activities, BEEP links black college students with successful black professionals who can share their knowledge and experience about succeeding in the work world.

As the program's director, Du Jean, a self-admitted, self-mocking "know-it-all," is always on the go, making sure that everything at BEEP runs smoothly. And that's no small task. Under her leadership BEEP has gained the cooperation of more than eight hundred corporations, government agencies, and professional organizations, and some four thousand high-level black executives and professionals, who have worked together to help an estimated six hundred thousand students nationwide. By creating opportunities for black professionals to teach in colleges and other settings, BEEP aims to "close the gap between classroom experiences and the real world of work." BEEP schools students on topics rarely found in a traditional curriculum.

It's a fitting role for someone whose life can hardly be described as traditional. Besides a work schedule that keeps her traveling 65 percent of the time, Du Jean puts 100 percent of herself into numerous outside projects, from the YMCA to serving as an advisor to the Miss America Organization.

Using what she describes as her "hyperactive" style, Du Jean pushes herself, and everyone who works with her, for one reason: "I *care*," she said. "I care *a lot*. I'm not driven by money. If I was, I'd be at a profit-making institution. And there have been a *lot* of overtures made. At the National Urban League, I deal with young people. That's what I care about, being involved and making a difference in the lives of others."

Along the way, she's also made news. She was a columnist for *The Daily Challenge,* New York's first black newspaper. Her work with BEEP has been recognized with numerous honors: she was awarded an honorary doctor of laws degree by Morris College in Sumter, South Carolina; named Visiting Professor by more than thirty colleges and universities; and given a presidential commendation from Jimmy Carter, to name a few. Her influence has been instrumental in setting up meetings abroad between America's black business executives and Caribbean businessmen, govern-

Renee Du Jean

ment officials, members of Parliament, and a prime minister or two.

All this has proved valuable training for her latest venture: in July 1992, at age 57, Du Jean became a first-time, single working mother when she adopted a six-year-old boy from Jamaica.

Motherhood offered Du Jean "a whole new lifestyle," one that made dealing with presidents and prime ministers seem like a cinch, she said. Not surprisingly, one priority on her parenting agenda has been getting her son to read.

It is a personal passion she inherited from her father, a law student and a self-made businessman. When Du Jean was little more than a toddler, her father pointed her toward the bookshelf. Her first lessons were learning the ABCs; then she graduated to the dictionary.

"I had to get ten words each day out of the dictionary and explain them and spell them," she said. Next on the family's "required reading list" were law books and the Bible.

One of her most valued possessions as a child was her library card because it opened so many worlds for her. "I read about *every-thing*," she recalled. From fairy tales and folklore from around the globe to biology and botany, the knowledge Du Jean hungered for was just a book or a chapter or a page away. By the time she reached her freshman year in high school, she said, "I knew *so* much."

Some of what she knew didn't exactly please her dad: Superman and Clark Kent were the same person; Blondie was smarter than her husband, Dagwood Bumstead; Spiderman could always be counted on to save the day. Comic books were the one form of reading her father forbade. But that didn't discourage the feisty Du Jean; she would just sneak them into the house.

But as a kid, Du Jean could hardly be cast as a reclusive book-worm. She found plenty of time to play with her brothers and cousins. Together, they were a lively and imaginative bunch.

"We were all leaders," Du Jean recalled. "We were all assertive. We always came up with plays and talent shows." They even took their show on the road, singing, acting, and dancing for family friends — the judges and businesspeople her father was associated with.

These childhood performances prepared Du Jean for life. With the freedom to be creative and applause for her efforts, "it was almost impossible *not* to be motivated," she said. "It helped to make me feel that if I wanted to do anything, I could."

If it was money she wanted, she would have to work for it — those were her mother's orders. That was simple enough, since her mother owned a small factory that produced housecoats. Du Jean learned to operate a sewing machine and began bringing home her own pay.

"I didn't have an allowance," she recalled. "I earned my money."

But when it came time to apply to college, Du Jean found she hadn't earned enough. "I was afraid to tell my mother about the money that was required to go to college," she said. So instead, Du Jean came up with a little lie: that she just wasn't going to go.

At the time, neither Du Jean nor her parents—who had split up when she was 11—knew anything about scholarships.

It wasn't until 1960 that Du Jean got her chance to go to college. She was working as a receptionist for the University Settlement House. Spotting untapped potential, Du Jean's employer gave her the money she needed for school.

She was finally on her way. Or so it seemed.

She had enrolled at New York's City College as a liberal arts major, but somehow, the school goofed and listed her as an engineering major. That meant that she had to take calculus. And that meant disaster.

"I sat in the front row to better hear and understand the professor. And seeing my quizzical look, the professor would ask, 'Miss Du Jean, do you understand?' "

"No," she most often replied. "I felt as though I was in kindergarten," she said, "and that they were speaking in a foreign tongue. I struggled. I *really* struggled. I was up nights. I tried just to get a passing grade."

When the dreaded *D* came in, she was crushed and quit school. After being an *A* student from first grade through several college courses, Du Jean said, "I couldn't bear the idea that I had failed."

Looking back, she realizes she was much too hard on herself. She didn't take into account the fact that she was still working full time while attending night classes full time. She also didn't realize something very important about herself: that she was a "morning person," someone whose brain power dimmed with the setting of the sun.

All she knew at the time was that she felt like a failure. That D grade defied every lesson she'd ever learned as a child. Her father had taught her, "If you're going to do anything, do it right the first time."

Today, she admits that's one lesson she's worked very hard to *unlearn.* Calling herself "dictatorial," Du Jean, who regularly juggles dozens and dozens of responsibilities with ease, struggles with learning how to be more flexible.

"In terms of my learning and development, that's certainly an area

I'm aware of," she said. "I still like things done right the first time. It saves so much time. But if it's not, I do understand—*if* I'm given a reason."

At times when life seems to take an unexpected bad turn for no good reason, Du Jean relies on her religious faith to see her through. Coming from a family of Jehovah's Witnesses, Seventh Day Adventists, Episcopalians, and Catholics, she said she's "gone through a number of religions," and every one has helped her.

"My faith is strong and I know that if I have a problem, all I have to do is go to my creator and ask Him to help me with it," she said. "I'd be so confused if I did not have something as stable as faith."

With a whirlwind schedule that seems to change from moment to moment, a job that requires long hours and lots of dashing from city to city to deal with top professionals, plus one endearing, but precocious little boy who can demand Herculean energy from his mom, Du Jean has her hands full. But that doesn't stop her from dreaming and setting goals, some new, and at least one that is many decades old.

BEEP has been a big part of Du Jean's life since 1969, when she joined the program as a research writer. Working her way up to director, she has dedicated countless hours to the task of ensuring that today's youth have every opportunity for the best educations possible.

All of which makes it especially ironic that the bright kid who was reading the newspaper before she entered first grade never completed her education. Not that she ever stopped learning—Du Jean did give college a second try, and she's taken many courses throughout adulthood. But she's yet to earn her own college degree.

"That's the one thing I have to overcome," she said.

"I have an honorary doctorate and have received many accolades, awards, and citations from various colleges. But I still don't have that degree. And that's something I will have to take care of. It's unfinished business.

"Even at this stage of my life."

Marian Wright Edelman

★ | *We cry and we sing and we pray. And then we get up, and we keep on fighting.*

Marian Wright Edelman has spent most of her life battling oppression and injustice.

At 52, she is best known as the founder and president of the Children's Defense Fund (CDF), an organization in Washington, D.C., that goes to bat for America's disadvantaged children and their families.

An eloquent speaker and author, Edelman has won widespread support by challenging some of the nation's most powerful and influential people to consider CDF's cause: "Our goal has been to encourage the country to invest in children and their families before they get sick, before they drop out of school, before they get pregnant."

Whether the issue is hunger, housing, urban violence — or any number of other problems that threaten young people — Edelman can cite facts and figures that add up to an alarming message passionately delivered.

"I can't stand the thought that innocent children who are voiceless are not going to have their needs attended to," she said. "The very fate of this country rests on what we do for our children today."

CDF, which celebrates its twentieth anniversary in 1993, was born out of Edelman's experiences as a Southern lawyer and civil rights activist. But the roots of CDF's social conscience and its protection of the powerless can be traced to Edelman's childhood in Bennettsville, South Carolina.

"I come out of a deep tradition of self-help," Edelman said. "Black folk have been helping themselves all their lives — that's all they had because they couldn't look to anybody else.

65

"The values that I was taught by my parents are that life is about service—and that service is the rent you pay for living, not something you do in your spare time."

The youngest of five children, Edelman grew up believing that good people can make a difference. "While the world had a lot problems—and black folks had an extra lot of problems—we were taught that we could struggle and change them," she said.

Equally important, Edelman was schooled in her values by people who "lived what they preached." Her mother, a community activist, ran a home for the elderly; her father was a Baptist preacher who believed in community service. "Working for the community was as much a part of our existence as eating and sleeping and church," she said.

In Bennettsville, blacks were not allowed at the local soda fountains. "So my daddy built a canteen behind our church so the black kids would have a place to go," Edelman said. "It was living Christianity."

Edelman's childhood also was influenced by "watching people who didn't have a whole lot, but boy, did they have dignity and strength. They were never bitter. These were ordinary folks of grace who were joyful. I always wanted to be as good as they were."

Injustice was part of life in her small, rural, segregated Southern hometown. Childhood incidents, such as of the black boy who stepped on a nail and died because no doctor would treat him, helped shape the beliefs that guide Edelman today.

"Things were not wonderful when I was growing up," Edelman said. "But what was important was that I had preachers and teachers and parents who were always there, telling me what was important, telling me that what was going on in the world was not about *me*— it was about *them*."

Her parents stressed higher education. Planning a foreign service career, Edelman attended Spelman College in Atlanta, Georgia. She graduated valedictorian of her class, but her career goals changed when the civil rights movement ignited.

During her senior year, Edelman participated in one of the largest sit-ins in Atlanta. She was one of fourteen students arrested, an experience that convinced her to attend law school—because civil rights lawyers were scarce and sorely needed. In 1960, she won a scholarship to Yale Law School.

Marian Wright Edelman   Photo: Rick Reinhard

During spring break of her final year of law school, Edelman went
to Mississippi to help with a voter registration drive led by her friend,
Robert Moses, for the Student Nonviolent Coordinating Committee
(SNCC). On her third and last day there, while helping Moses take

a group of people to the courthouse to register, she had one of the most frightening experiences of her life.

Moses was "at the head of that scraggly bunch of courageous people," Edelman recalled. "I was at the end of the line, behind an old man on crutches.

"The cops came with the dogs, and led them to attack us. I remember seeing a dog jump on Bob Moses and tear his pants, then it was just a terrifying scene—people running away, Bob and the other SNCC kids getting arrested, and throwing me their car keys as they were being led off," Edelman said.

"This was the first time I'd seen police dogs in action, and I've been scared of them ever since. If I see a German shepherd on the street, to this day I'll cross over to avoid him."

That summer was the first of many experiences in Mississippi that would direct the course of Edelman's life. The turbulent sixties not only advanced her career but deepened her conviction "that when you see a need you try to respond."

After finishing law school, Edelman returned to Mississippi, this time in an internship program that encouraged young lawyers to work in the South. One of the first two lawyers chosen for the internship sponsored by the National Association for the Advancement of Colored People (NAACP), Edelman trained for a year in New York City before heading south.

In the spring of 1964, she opened a law office in Jackson, Mississippi, to support civil rights efforts there. Her practice consisted mostly of getting students out of jail. But she couldn't practice law officially at first—because Mississippi required nonresidents to live there for a year before applying to the state bar. So Edelman made an arrangement with the three black lawyers in town to handle the paperwork she needed to get people out of jail.

There were hundreds of arrests and many violent episodes that summer. "I very seldom got a client out of jail who had not been beaten, who didn't have bones broken or teeth missing," she recalled.

"One young boy I represented had been shot and killed in jail, and I had to take his parents to the funeral home to view the body. It was another of those watershed experiences—I had nightmares for weeks, but afterward I felt I could face anything."

At age 26, Edelman became the first black woman to pass the bar in Mississippi. All the while, she was continuing her civil rights crusade: from 1964 to 1968, she ran the NAACP Legal Defense and Education Fund in Mississippi. And she helped win a grant to bring the Head Start program to the state.

But perhaps the most important thing to happen during those years was that Edelman came to the realization that in order to change things in Mississippi, she had to influence federal policy. "I began to understand that unless you put social and economic underpinnings under people, political and civil rights would be hollow," she said.

In 1968, she moved to Washington and, with federal grant money, began researching ways to aid the poor nationally. That was a difficult year for the civil rights movement. In April, Martin Luther King was assassinated; Robert Kennedy was shot two months later.

But it also was a time of joy: in July, Marian Wright married Peter Edelman, a white, Jewish Harvard Law School graduate and one of Robert Kennedy's legislative assistants. Many people in the civil rights movement saw their union as an optimistic sign in pessimistic times.

The couple had met in Mississippi the year before when Kennedy and staff members came to learn about hunger. Marian showed them shacks without heat, water, or light—and children who were sick and painfully malnourished.

The Edelmans left Washington in 1971, and moved to Boston, where she became director of the Harvard University Center for Law and Education.

Then in 1973, Marian began the work that has been her passion for two decades: she founded CDF, effectively becoming the voice of America's children. CDF was created to provide systematic and long-range assistance to children—and to ensure that their needs are a matter of national policy.

It is a mission that took root in Mississippi when Edelman witnessed what can happen when people get the help they truly need. The Head Start program "served thirteen thousand poor children, and gave three thousand poor parents training and comprehensive health services. And they began to get a new vision of the future," Edelman said.

"I watched what that program meant for children and began to see them have a new sense of possibility. And poor parents were empowered to work together, to make sure that their kids had a better life than they had."

The experience convinced her that only when people have their basic needs met can they begin to build dreams.

"It's hard to have strong values if you don't have a shelter over your head and you don't have any support in your community," she said. "We have to give people housing and food and jobs so that they can do what they want to with their kids.

"That's key—and that's why I moved to Washington, to see if I couldn't protect programs like Head Start, to fight the politicians who were trying to undermine what the parents were trying to do."

Under Edelman's leadership, CDF has been a powerful advocate, influencing legislation and raising public awareness on issues ranging from child health to youth employment to family support systems.

One of CDF's chief concerns is teenage pregnancy—because it is both a major cause and effect of poverty. "It is our view that the best way to prevent teenage pregnancies is to give young people a sense of hope," says Edelman. "A sense that they have a future."

While other organizations emphasize caring for the unwed mother and providing services for the child, CDF tries to prevent these pregnancies and all their attendant social handicaps before they occur.

Edelman also is deeply concerned about the fate of young families. She's outraged that the most this nation's leadership seems to be able to do is spout empty rhetoric about family values.

"The fact is, this country is hypocritical," Edelman said. "We talk family values and yet we don't support families. We don't back up what we preach with our deeds.

"Young families of all races trying to get off the ground today are having a heck of a hard time because of the decline in wages, the lack of jobs, and their inability to buy a house. We don't even give our families basic health insurance so that their children can get care when they get sick."

The ranks of the poor and underprivileged are growing at an alarming rate—and that affects everyone's future.

"These children are going to be critical to every American's standard of living and to the very ability of this country to compete in the twenty-first century," said Edelman. "America's competitiveness rests on what we do for these children. You may not like them, but if you're worried about taxes and money, it's cheaper to invest in nutrition, and immunization, and child care, than jailhouses."

During her early days in Washington, Edelman quickly learned how to get things done. She realized that if she picked issues that affected large numbers of children—white kids as well as black, middle class as well as poor—the poor would more likely get helped.

Over the years, her work has been praised by parents, politicians, and the press alike. As early as 1971, *Time Magazine* recognized her as one of America's two hundred young leaders; nineteen years later, *Ladies' Home Journal* named her one of America's fifty most powerful women.

Senator Edward Kennedy has called her the "101st senator for children's issues—she has a real power in Congress and uses it brilliantly." And in a 1990 article, *The Los Angeles Times* said, "Over the past twenty years, Edelman has become the most powerful advocate in America for children, a feared lobbyist demanding that the government provide the support the nation's young so desperately need."

Even now, Edelman is still so driven that when she speaks on her pet issues, she doesn't even pause to punctuate her sentences—the words tumble out in a rush. Some people are simply overwhelmed, not only by her rapid-fire delivery, but by a content that is dizzying. She is still the preacher's daughter serving the community, only now it's expanded to the whole country.

The energetic Edelman typically works twelve-hour days. Her plant-filled office hints of life outside work—running shoes under a chair, posters of Italy, and photographs of her family. The Edelmans have three sons, whom they raised in the dual traditions of his Judaism and her Christianity.

"We wanted them to know what brings us together is much greater than what divides us," Edelman said.

They ran their household with the help of a housekeeper from Edelman's hometown. But even with that kind of support, being a working mother has not been easy: "I, who have everything, am hanging on by my fingernails," Edelman said. "I don't know how poor women manage."

When Edelman's oldest son turned 21, she wanted to find something meaningful she could give her children to mark their passage into adulthood.

"I realized there's this psychic tape that goes off in my head in every situation," Edelman said. "I instinctively say, now what would Daddy do here, what would Mama say?"

Appreciating what clear internal anchors her parents had given her, Edelman hoped she had done the same for her children. "But just in case," she said, "I decided to write what I valued most because my children are growing up in a more complicated time."

She wrote her sons a letter, which turned into her latest book, *The Measure of Our Success: A Letter to My Children and Yours*. The book's lessons underscore the themes of Edelman's life:

> Be decent and fair and insist that others be so in your presence.
> Be a quiet servant-leader and example in your home, school, workplace, and community.
> It doesn't matter how many times you fall down. What matters is how many times you get up."

Besides this book, Edelman is the author of four others, plus numerous articles.

Edelman believes her life has been enriched by learning the values of unselfish living at a very young age. "The legacies that parents and church and teachers left to my generation of black children were priceless but not material: a living faith reflected in daily service, the discipline of hard work and stick-to-it-iveness, and a capacity to struggle," she wrote to her sons.

"Giving up and 'burnout' were not part of the language of my elders—you got up every morning and you did what you had to do and you got up every time you fell down and tried as many times as you had to to get it done right."

Edelman expects nothing less of herself, of her country, and of future generations. Twenty years of preaching the same message and pushing for reform have not weakened her resolve—if anything, she's grown more passionate in her call to action.

"Every single American—black, white, Latino—can make a difference to a child," Edelman said. "You can find time to mentor, to tutor. You can give a little money to give them a chance to go off to a camp. You can give them a summer job. You can write a letter on their behalf.

"We each can make a difference. We can teach our children to be fair and decent. We can teach them to be tolerant by not laughing at racial jokes or gender jokes," she said.

"We must show our children this is a can-do country that can bring itself together again—our best days have got to be ahead of us."

Joseph Fernandez

 If you reach for the sky and tell kids what you're reaching for, a lot of them will reach with you.

Joseph Fernandez was a high school dropout. In the early fifties, as a street-smart Puerto Rican kid, he was a messenger at New York City's Board of Education in Brooklyn. Nearly four decades later, he returned — as chancellor of the country's largest and most troubled school system.

Fernandez hit his hometown streets running when he accepted the job in January 1990. In a rush of publicity — bearing such head-lines as "Can a Former Dropout Save New York's Schools?" — he boldly vowed to make changes that would "turn the system on its head." For too long, he said, New York's public schools had failed to provide their students with decent educations.

It had failed Fernandez as well.

Raised in Spanish Harlem, in a crowded six-story walk-up apartment, Fernandez, like many city kids, did a lot of his growing up on the streets. He loved athletics, especially football, and was known as a tough quarterback who didn't avoid physical contact.

"He always wanted to jump on you in the hallways of the tenements," said a boyhood friend, now a U.S. customs agent.

Briefly aspiring to be a priest, Fernandez went to a Roman Catholic high school. But the boy changed, along with his neighborhood, when drugs and gangs began to take over life in Harlem. Fernandez joined The Riffs, a sporting group that got into after-game scuffles. The right side of his nose is still scarred from the time a rival gang member smashed it with a Pepsi sign.

By his own account, Fernandez was far from a model student: "My day consisted of getting up in the morning, saying good-bye to my parents, telling them I was going to school, getting on the subway, meeting by Columbus Circle with a group of guys and gals, and going down to 42nd Street."

In fact, he rarely even bothered to check in at school—and remembers spending more time at the movies than in classrooms. Once, a week-long absence left him and some friends in a jam. But they cleverly escaped punishment: "We didn't have any excuse, so we put calamine lotion on our faces and said we had poison ivy," Fernandez recalled.

Such antics eventually caught up with him, and Fernandez was kicked out of high school. At his next school, he didn't behave much better. His backside was regularly paddled by the dean of discipline. The best thing in his life was his girlfriend, Lily Pons.

Then he began hanging out with heroin addicts and petty thieves, and by 1952, Fernandez was just another seventeen-year-old drop-out on the streets of Harlem.

Like most of his friends, Fernandez became involved in drugs; he clearly was in the wrong crowd. A good friend went to jail for holding up a subway token booth. Another one got stabbed in a bar and died. A couple he knew overdosed on heroin.

Fernandez realized he had to get off the city's streets. He told his parents he was joining the air force. They didn't like the idea, and tried to talk him out of it.

"If you don't sign the papers, I will go anyway," Fernandez told them. "This neighborhood is no good, and I want to get out of here."

The service proved to be "the big turning point" for Fernandez. He trained as a radio technician, did tours in Japan and Korea, and earned his high school equivalency diploma.

Returning home, Fernandez capped his five-year engagement by marrying Lily Pons, and used the GI Bill to enroll at Columbia University, where his mother had once worked as a maid. He got hooked on the "new math," taught by Sidney Meyer Levin, a pioneer in the field.

"He just orchestrated that class," said Fernandez. "The guy was like a maestro."

Meanwhile, the couple had a child, who developed a bad case of croup. When their doctor suggested that a warmer climate might help their son's health, the Fernandezes closed their $800 savings account, packed up their belongings and their collie, and drove to Miami, Florida.

There Fernandez worked his way through college as a postman and milkman. He earned a bachelor's degree in education from the University of Miami in 1963.

That year he took a job teaching math at Coral Park High School. "The first day I became a teacher I knew I wanted to be principal," he said. Within a year, he was promoted to department chairman.

From the moment he stepped into the classroom, it was clear Fernandez had a way with kids.

One student, Steven Reinemund, signed Fernandez's 1966 yearbook: "I can't tell you how much you have meant to me for the last three years. Since I have not had a father, I have respected your opinion in matters as I would have respected my father's." Reinemund is now chief executive officer of Pizza Hut.

Fernandez had plenty of fathering to do at home as well; he and his wife had three more children, one boy and two girls. Taking extra jobs to supplement his teaching income, he worked as a union steward and tutored kids at home. He also continued his college education, earning his master's degree from Florida Atlantic University in 1970.

All the while, his career was advancing steadily. In 1971, he became an assistant high school principal. Four years later, at age 39, Fernandez got his first big chance to demonstrate his innovative style of leadership. He was assigned the principalship at Miami Central Senior High, a predominantly black school located in a Dade County slum.

At the time, there were no black department heads at Central. Fernandez changed that—and a lot of other things. He put an end to kids with blasting radios hanging around after classes. And he kept in touch with students by teaching a 7:30 A.M. math class.

At home, remembering his own experiences as a student, Fernandez set mandatory study hours for his children. "He had come from a family that was very poor and uneducated," said his son Keith. "He didn't want me to struggle the way his family had to."

Fernandez's ascent up the academic ladder continued. In 1985, he was appointed Dade County assistant superintendent. That year, he

Joseph Fernandez

also received his doctoral degree in education from Nova University in Fort Lauderdale. The following year, he was promoted to deputy superintendent.

Equally important, he became the head of a task force that developed the controversial program for which he is best known: school-based management.

Simply put, the program aims to minimize bureaucracy by giving the people who work in the schools the power to run them. Fernandez has described the program this way: "Teachers, parents, and administrators participate in decision-making about budgets, staff, curriculum, and scheduling in their schools.

"Schools are able to implement ideas they could only dream about in the past. The only limit they now face is their own creativity."

Similarly, Fernandez set no limits on his own growth. In 1987, he accepted what would prove to be the pivotal post in his career—superintendent of Dade County, the nation's fourth-largest school system.

Fernandez's reign at Dade County is legend. One of the better-known stories tells how he paid a surprise visit to an unsuspecting principal.

Superintendent Fernandez had been on the job about a month when he decided to stop by an elementary school in a poor neighborhood. He couldn't believe what he found: trash was scattered all over the schoolyard; the grass was overgrown; windows were broken everywhere; and the bathrooms were so filthy the toilets were stinking up the whole school.

Dropping by the principal's office, Fernandez found him watching a TV soap opera. "Pack up and get out of here," Fernandez ordered.

That story raced through the ranks of employees—and the moral of the tale was not lost: one principal was later seen mowing the grass at his school on a Sunday.

Nicknamed "Joltin' Joe," Fernandez, by some accounts, revolutionized education in Dade County. This much is certain: in the space of two years, he removed or transferred forty-eight principals; started Saturday computer and music classes at many schools; gave pep talks to eighteen thousand teachers; and raised unprecedented amounts of money. Thanks to Fernandez's hard sell and a positive word-of-mouth campaign, school-based management was adopted by about half of Miami's schools.

Reaction to the innovative management program remains mixed, but Fernandez is pleased by the change it encouraged. "They are happy schools," he said. "Teachers literally have been freed to be teachers. It's their plan, their strategy, their dollars. As you get ownership, my experience has been, people try a little bit harder to make the thing work."

But critics don't see it that way. Some parents feel Fernandez's approach gives too much power to the teachers. "They give lip service to parents," said one, citing the example of how, at one Miami school, teachers turned a room into a "wellness lounge" with exercise equipment for themselves.

Just the same, the pioneering work he was doing in Florida was making a name for Fernandez in the nation's academic circles. So when New York City Schools Chancellor Richard Green suddenly died, the legendary Fernandez was considered the logical candidate for the post. The Board of Education began trying to woo him to New York.

Fernandez agonized over the move and its impact on his career. But there was no question that the New York City job was the top of the ladder he had been climbing for twenty-five years. New York Public Schools sweetened the offer with a $40,000 raise and a Brooklyn Heights brownstone, which will be used by future chancellors as well. Fernandez agreed to accept what one New York official described as "the toughest job in America in education."

Chancellor Fernandez found that out in a hurry. While he'd had no trouble getting things moving in Miami, almost everything in his hometown was hard. Procedures and red tape stalled even the most routine requests: it took him weeks to receive yellow highlighting pens and months to get his dirty office windows cleaned.

But the energetic Fernandez was not deterred. "We're trying to bring New York City into the twentieth century—forget the twenty-first!"

It's a big job. Fernandez inherited a school system desperately in need of strong leadership and suffering an alarming array of problems, among them: a twenty-seven percent dropout rate; overcrowded classrooms with shattered windows, broken lights, leaking roofs, and busted toilets; teachers spending their own money on supplies; a fifth-grader arrested with 411 vials of crack; and a kindergartner carrying a handgun to class.

79

In the face of such overwhelming odds, some people questioned whether the school system could be fixed. "It's doable," the no-nonsense Fernandez promised. "Maybe not over a year or two. But it can be done. The danger I face as chancellor is that all the improvements won't happen overnight. My role is one of a catalyst, to set the direction we want to go in."

Fernandez began making news the moment he took office. Calling the school system "Fat City," he cut four hundred jobs from a staff of five thousand. He took cars away from fourteen Board of Education bureaucrats. He announced that he wanted to change laws that guaranteed principals their jobs, whether they were competent or not.

On his second day in office, Fernandez began visiting schools in the worst slums. Followed by reporters, he asked why there were no after-school programs and if teachers got to make decisions. Right away, the teachers and students knew they had a friend.

Dropping in on a class, he introduced himself to the teacher, who told her eight-year-olds, "This is Dr. Joseph Fernandez. He is going to do some great and fantastic things. You'll be seeing him on the news."

A black girl in the front row raised her hand and asked which station he'd be on.

"I'll tell you what, I'll make sure you get in the paper," Fernandez said, giving her a hug as the cameras flashed. The next day, their embrace made the front page of *The New York Times.*

A man with a mission, Fernandez has proven he is not afraid to make controversial decisions. Even though he's Catholic, he persuaded the city's school board to hand out a flyer explaining AIDS. And he pushed for distribution of condoms in public schools, saying, "We cannot put our heads in the sand."

Fernandez has a long list of improvements he's working on. He wants New York's schools to play a leading role in the struggle against drugs and racial tension. He wants to see more minority teachers as role models in a student body that is about 80 percent African-American, Hispanic, and Asian.

He's pushing for innovative reforms that truly address the needs of today's students and remove obstacles to their success. For example, aware that many children must work to help support their poor families, Fernandez has suggested that schools respond accordingly by offering evening and weekend classes.

"The traditional thinking is that schools are open from nine to three and that's it," he said. "I don't buy it.

"We need to change these structures to meet the needs of the students—instead of trying to change the kids to meet the structure."

If Fernandez has anything to say about it, today's students won't follow his example and drop out.

"We have the potential to lose a whole generation of kids unless we do something, quickly," Fernandez said.

He wants to give them the dreams he didn't have: "If you reach for the sky and tell kids what you're reaching for, a lot of them will reach with you."

Confident he can revitalize New York's public schools, Fernandez won't settle for less.

"I'm very impatient with incompetence," he said. "I'm very impatient with people who don't want to try things differently, who say things can't be done because we've never tried it that way before."

This fast-talking New Yorker has not endeared himself to everyone with his hard-line approach. While supporters applaud his fierce determination and describe him as a charismatic champion of long-overdue changes in the city schools, critics regard him as brash, and his measures harsh.

Fernandez seems unfazed by the constant debate. "I'll never be able to satisfy anybody in anything if I do what's popular and not what's right."

But on one point critics and supporters do agree: no chancellor before him has brought more energy and dedication to the job. Fernandez is routinely at his desk by 7 A.M. and rarely leaves the office until the clock strikes 7 again. But that's nothing new—he kept the same schedule when he was responsible for fifty students, rather than one million.

Though Fernandez, now 56, may be at the pinnacle of his career, he's hardly in an enviable position. New York is a tough town, and his job has been known to chew people up.

But the spirited chancellor welcomes the challenge—because if he succeeds in rebuilding New York's schools, it will send a message to cities around the country.

"The road to improving schools is a long and difficult one," he said. "But good schools are what I'm after.

"Five years from now, I want New York's school system to be one of the best in the U.S."

George C. Fraser

Life is about happiness, and happiness includes the self-respect that comes from accepting responsibility for one's life and earning one's way in the world. We have all the tools we need, right here, right now. We must be willing to share our success and help others succeed.

Entrepreneur George C. Fraser believes one of the best ways for blacks to succeed is to learn from each other. Blacks, he said, must tap into the "intellectual capital"—the tremendous resources and talent—available within their own communities. But too often, that intellectual capital isn't drawn upon or reinvested in the people who need it most.

That's why Fraser created *SuccessGuides,* professional directories designed to link blacks across the country, and ultimately, across the world.

"The most important responsibility we have as black people is to succeed, to succeed in spite of racism, to succeed in spite of drugs, to succeed in spite of the odds against us," Fraser said. "Our forefathers succeeded in the face of greater odds. It is our turn now, and we are much better prepared. We must not, and cannot, and will not fail them."

Fraser launched his first *SuccessGuide* in 1988 in Cleveland, Ohio. Numbering 224 pages, the handbook listed three thousand black executives, lawyers, doctors, nurses, high school principals—even caterers—in the metropolitan area. The guide was the first of its kind in the United States. More than five thousand copies were sold.

Encouraged by initial sales, Fraser began doing annual updates in Cleveland and expanding the guide to other cities. By 1991, he was introducing guides in six other cities: New York, Detroit, Cincinnati,

83

Chicago, Atlanta, and Washington, D.C. And he plans to expand the directories to Baltimore, Dallas, Houston, Los Angeles, Memphis, and Philadelphia.

"The guides are a way for black people to connect," Fraser said. "They are a productive and effective way to link people together and enhance the images and visibility of black entrepreneurs and professionals. *SuccessGuide* aims to identify role models not by tens, but by the thousands.

"Our goal is to publish twenty-five *SuccessGuides* all across America and link together over one million top black professionals and entrepreneurs by 1995. By 1997, we also will include West Africa, the United Kingdom, the Caribbean, and Canada. Can you imagine the importance and power of one million black people talking to each other?"

A strong entrepreneurial drive and a commitment to helping others are Fraser's trademarks.

SuccessGuide is the centerpiece of his marketing and media company, SuccessSource Inc., a company built on the theme "Linking people and ideas." In addition to the guides, Fraser has created a nationally syndicated radio show called "For Your Success," and professional forums for blacks called SuccessNet. The radio show, which Fraser hosts, is heard daily in seventy-five markets. The program features motivational interviews with outstanding black professionals.

Fraser also has started a nonprofit organization called the National Institute for the Study and Development of Black Excellence. The organization's mission is to freely provide inner-city black youths nationwide with the products and services of SuccessSource.

The birth of such ideas can be traced to Fraser's boyhood in Brooklyn, New York. He was born in 1945, the youngest in a family of nine kids. But for much of his childhood, Fraser was separated from his six brothers and two sisters.

"My mother became mentally ill while I was a baby and my father, who was a cab driver, could not take care of nine children," Fraser recalled. "So we were all sort of carted off in threes to foster homes."

Fraser credits his foster parents with providing the "foundation and influence of most of my beliefs." Solid folks who valued education and excellence, "[they] were very hard-working people," Fraser

George Fraser

said, "and they made us work very hard. Even with small projects around the home — if they were not done right, they were repeated until they were.

"I hated it while I was a child, but I think that in retrospect it has paid off."

Fraser and his siblings were reunited in his mid-teens, and they remain close today. "We certainly had some trials and tribulations growing up, but we all turned out to be pretty solid citizens," Fraser said. For instance, one brother is in Africa starting a business, and a sister who graduated from Harvard holds an administrative post with the New York public schools.

"I'm pretty proud of the family and the spectrum of our accomplishments," he said.

One reason for their success, Fraser believes, is the experience of growing up in the working-class black neighborhood of Bedford-Stuyvesant, where "there was a very great sense of family in the entire community. It was very much like the African proverb that says, 'It takes a village to raise a child.' "

Fraser remembers that "If you went down the block, although you weren't in eyesight of your parents, if you were within eyesight of anybody who knew your parents, you'd better behave—or it would get back to your parents. Or they would take action into their own hands."

More importantly, as a kid he never had to look far for role models. "I mean the physician and the dentist and the attorneys lived down the block, and the grocery stores were around the corner," he recalled. "I had a whole bunch of role models, from the minister to the barber in the barbershop.

"So that helped—and that's the thing that's missing in urban America."

City kids today have little or no exposure to successful middle-class blacks. "Most of us who benefited from the civil rights laws enacted in the sixties have gotten educations, climbed the corporate ladder, or started our own business, and have basically moved away from the inner city," Fraser said.

And there's little opportunity for kids to be exposed to positive role models, as he was, Fraser said, because mainstream media focuses on blacks involved in welfare, crime, or drugs, "or when we can sing or dance or play football, baseball, or basketball."

For Fraser, that signals an opportunity and a responsibility for successful black professionals to "go back to those communities and serve ourselves up as role models.

"The battlefield that we as African-Americans are going to have to fight on in the future will be the battlefield of excellence, quality, and competitiveness," he said. "I have found that after forty-seven years, where there is excellence, quality, and competitiveness, racism tends to be less of an issue. It's when you are not about excellence, quality, and competitiveness, and you are an African-American in this country, that you have a serious problem."

Long before Fraser started SuccessSource, he was building a reputation as a talented businessperson and energetic community leader.

A graduate of Dartmouth College, he gained some of his earliest business know-how as a marketing manager for the consumer products giant Procter & Gamble. In a twelve-year career there, he earned the title of Manager of the Year four times. He left Procter & Gamble in 1984 to become director of marketing and communications for United Way Services of Cleveland.

At United Way, Fraser's work again drew attention: he was written up in *The Guiness Book of World Records* for releasing more than one and a half million balloons over Cleveland to launch the city's 1986 United Way campaign. The record still stands.

Fraser said he developed the idea "to demonstrate to everyone that when people work together you can make the impossible possible."

In recognition of his contributions to the community, Cleveland created "George C. Fraser Day" on February 29, 1992, and gave him the key to the city. He also was named Black Professional of the Year for 1992 by the Black Professionals Association of Cleveland.

These honors are the most recent in a long and diverse list of accomplishments marking his career and community service. In 1991, he became the first black to appear on the cover of Continental Airlines' in-flight magazine; he was named Role Model of the Year in 1988 in the Teen Father Program; in 1985, the Ohio Senate and House of Representatives commended him for outstanding community service; and he was the United Negro College Fund's Volunteer of the Year in 1982 and 1983.

Besides his community activities, Fraser serves on the boards of ten professional organizations, including the Black Professionals Association Foundation and the Greater Cleveland Growth Association.

Fraser's many years of business experience and community involvement have united in his latest venture, SuccessSource. Through his company, Fraser is reaching out to his fellow black professionals and preaching the gospel of responsibility—a message that urges the successful to give back some of what they have achieved in order to help their own communities.

"We must mobilize and motivate the black middle class to get involved. It is in our best interest," he said, noting that there are nearly two million blacks in executive, managerial, supervisory, and professional specialty positions in the United States.

"In real life, there is no single success greater than the team," Fraser said. "And we no longer have the luxury of being independent. We cannot have thirty-one million negroes running around here doing their own thing. We must become interdependent, linked together in a human bond of caring and sharing.

"As long as there is one black person on welfare, living in a housing project, or denied a quality education, we are all there. Every culture in America understands that and acts on it but us!"

Fraser fervently believes that blacks possess the power and talent to overcome their own problems. He espouses the credo of individual responsibility, not government handouts. "Government cannot give you happiness," he said. "It can only ensure the conditions under which you can pursue it for yourself."

Fraser readily acknowledges that many black Americans are in a state of crisis. "We must return to and embrace excellence, self-help, education, family, God, and community," he said.

It is his belief in the power and the potential of the black community to nurture its own that inspired Fraser to create SuccessSource and *SuccessGuides*.

"Our history tells us that we have built pyramids, and solved complex engineering problems when other cultures were living in huts," he said. "Today, we are the most educated and professionally trained generation of Africans in the history of the world. Surely we have the network and skills to solve our own problems. I suggest we stop talking about it and just do it."

For his part, Fraser aims to practice what he preaches. He works hard to be the kind of person who inspires others to action, and has little patience for those who invest their energies in making excuses for why they can't do more.

"All the great thinkers throughout history agree that happiness flows from realizing your full human potential, through doing productive work and overcoming ever more challenging obstacles," he said. "The driving force must be your own inner goals rather than the mere need to make a living.

"It is now time to look racism squarely in the face and say: 'You can't stop me, this is my country, too, and my place is anywhere my talents will take me.' "

Johnnie Mae Gibson

★ *You can't look at someone and judge them by their outer appearance. You have to get to know a little more about that inner person. Give it some time to settle in.*

Johnnie Mae Gibson had gotten herself involved with stolen-art dealers and knew she could wind up dead. So the demure little lady did exactly what her boss had ordered. For days she waited in a room full of Spanish-speaking people and kept her mouth shut. No way was she leaving until she saw the cash. And the moment she had the money in hand, she reached for her gun.

"FBI," she announced. "You're under arrest."

That was the first undercover assignment Supervisory Special Agent Gibson ever performed for the FBI And it was the FBI's first opportunity to see what a determined black woman could accomplish—with very few words and no gunfire.

"I only knew how to say *'No habla español,'*" Gibson explained. That's why the FBI wouldn't allow her to speak. If the Hispanic dealers had caught on that she wasn't really one of "them"—that she couldn't even find her way to the bathroom in Spanish—she could have blown her cover, risking her career and, very possibly, several lives.

But Gibson, one of the first black women to become an agent in the FBI since its founding in 1908, isn't used to blowing anything.

"Driven" is the word people typically use to describe her, Gibson said. But that's not really how she sees herself. Rather, she said, "I'm never satisfied—I know that there's always something more I could be doing, or could be doing better."

Born in the small Florida town of Caryville in 1949, she was the baby girl in a family of seven kids.

But Gibson grew up fast, through circumstances and her parents' teachings. An independent youngster, she was forced to fend for herself after her mother became completely paralyzed giving birth to her seventh child, a son.

"The last time I saw my mother walk, I was 5 years old," Gibson said. "We children did not want her to want for nothing in the world."

Just the same, Gibson's mother played a powerful role in her upbringing, instilling values that have governed this Special Agent's life for years. Because of her mother's teachings, Gibson believed that if she failed or did anything immoral, "everybody would say that it was because of my mother's handicap — that she was not a good parent. She stressed that whatever I do, don't make her look bad. She didn't want to be the bearer of someone who failed.

"And that's all I needed," Gibson said. "Until the time she died, everything I did, I did bearing in mind that I didn't want her to get hurt."

Gibson's mother cautioned her four daughters to get educations and to learn to be more than wives and mothers. "Her main thing," Gibson said, "was that you should never be dependent on a man. So when times get rough, you can always go on."

It was a lesson delivered from the heart and learned the hard way: without an education herself, Gibson's mother wasn't only paralyzed, she was hopelessly stuck in an unhappy marriage to a strong-willed man who knew how to make a point.

One Thanksgiving when Gibson was a teenager, a white man for whom her father had fixed a radio stopped by with a turkey, an extra one that he didn't need — and that the Gibson family clearly couldn't afford. Would they please take it? he offered.

Standing on the front porch for the whole family to see, Gibson's father turned down the man's generosity. But the white man was not easily put off. Back and forth they went, the white man politely insisting, the black man politely refusing. Finally, Gibson begged her father to take the turkey. But with him, no meant NO.

Later on, she went to the gentleman and asked for the turkey, which she roasted golden brown. Hoping to surprise her family, she proudly brought the bird to the dinner table. Sure enough, it was a surprise. Her brothers and sisters watched in shock as their father bellowed, "Get that thing out of here now."

But the family was too stunned to move. So Gibson's father

grabbed the turkey and violently threw it to the floor.

"It was his way of trying to get it over to us children that you don't wait around for handouts—that you go out and make it," Gibson said. "Otherwise, you'll never excel to try to get anything better."

Though less harsh, her mother had a way of driving home the same message, Gibson said. "She stressed on a daily basis that my future was mine to hold, to accept and become whatever I wanted to be, as long as I was healthy."

With those teachings and a few personal belongings, Gibson set off for college. First she earned an associate degree in nursing at a small school nearby, and then went on to Albany State College in Georgia for her bachelor's degree.

It was there she met her first love. They married and he promised to give her the kind of life she had only seen in movies: a nice home, smart clothes, exotic vacations. Little did the young bride know it was the kind of promise just waiting to broken.

Not long after their wedding, Gibson graduated from Albany State College and got her first job as a physical education teacher at a local high school.

She soon became pregnant. The couple was just barely getting by and she realized she had to find another job fast. Everywhere she went, Gibson filled out applications. But as far as she could tell, they ended up in the trash—except for one. Just three weeks after her daughter, Tiffany, was born, Gibson was offered a job as an officer with the Albany, Georgia, Police Department.

"The timing was right," she said. "Afraid of being accused of sexual and racial discrimination, they needed to hire females, and I just happened to be looking for a job and I happened to be black."

But telling her husband about the job was a matter of even trickier timing. Though he'd known about her application to the police department, he hadn't taken it seriously, Gibson recalled. And she didn't think he'd be pleased with her new job.

So one day as they were sharing a romantic moment, and it seemed he was in good spirits, she decided to break the news. Telling him to close his eyes—because she had a surprise and needed to slip into a different outfit—she hurried into the bathroom and put on her new uniform. Proudly prancing into their bedroom, she came face-to-face with a furious husband. Seeing

Johnnie Mae Gibson

her in blue from head to toe was the last thing he'd expected.

"I had to take the job before asking him," Gibson said. "Otherwise, I never would have taken it. I knew that once he saw me in uniform, there was no turning back."

It wasn't that her husband was against having a working wife, he just couldn't see her as a cop. Packing a pistol and arresting people was strictly a man's job—especially a white man's. And besides, the

93

Gibsons' marriage was already in danger of breaking apart, what with the pressures of their family responsibilities and poor finances.

By her own account, Gibson was unprepared for the realities of police work. If anything, she had an outdated image of the job: she imagined herself as "Officer Friendly"—someone who directed traffic, helped children across the street, and stood tall in the community. But this was the early seventies, and officers were called "pigs."

As for danger in the line of duty, the new kid in uniform didn't have a clue. Drug busts? Domestic violence? Knifings? She couldn't envision herself in such situations. But after teaming up with an FBI agent to track down a man who had beaten, raped, and murdered a prostitute, Gibson began to see what it meant to earn a police paycheck.

In fact, the FBI was so impressed with Gibson's work on that case they asked her to join the agency. She agreed, in much the same way she had accepted the police department's offer: "I had no idea what the FBI did" before working on the prostitute's case, Gibson said. "And this was in 1976, to show you how sheltered I was."

But true to form, Gibson was a quick study. After an intensive four months at the FBI Academy in Quantico, Virginia, Gibson, at age 27, was wearing a new badge and packing her bags for Florida. Her first assignment was in Miami; today she's based in Detroit, where she's lived for almost four years, maintaining a long-distance marriage with her second husband, who works in Washington, D.C.

Much of Gibson's work, particularly early in her career, involved undercover assignments. She proved to be quite a good actress. And she loved trying on new roles.

"For the moment," she said, "you were somebody else—you had a new name and a new attitude."

Her favorite undercover job called for her to play a singer in a Los Angeles supper club. "I've always wanted to be a Billie Holiday, and even today, that's one of the things I'd love to be," she said. But she quickly laughs, as if to say she's not taking this whole business too seriously.

"I don't think I have the voice," she said. "But to sing in a supper club and have a piano player—that would be the greatest thing!"

Gibson may be underestimating her voice. A talent scout who happened to be in the audience during her undercover singing assignment offered Gibson and her partner a record contract. No thanks, they told the scout, never explaining that they were just pretending to be promising musicians.

While her experiences with the FBI have taught Gibson a lot, she hates some of what she's learned. As far as racism and sexism are concerned, the bureau isn't all that different from the rest of the world, she said. In some ways, it reminds her of her earliest days in college, when she first encountered white society. No matter how she dressed, no matter how hard she studied, Gibson was constantly reminded that she was black and didn't fit in. White classmates wouldn't even sit next to her on the bus; she felt as though she would always be at a disadvantage because others considered her an outsider.

Even after she had earned her master's degree, she continued to receive similar treatment from fellow police officers. Although the force granted her "a certain degree of respect," she said, some of the guys, guys who "didn't even have a third-grade education," always managed to discount her for the very things she'd always been most proud of: she was a woman, and a black woman at that.

Even with sixteen years of FBI experience behind her, Gibson reports pretty much the same story. Despite all the responsibilities she's handled and been honored for—leading investigations that caught corrupt officials and drug dealers; supervising the agency's Fugitive and Violent Crimes Program; earning several awards and being named an Honorary Kentucky Colonel—she still struggles with discrimination.

Even the fact that in 1986, CBS aired *Johnnie Gibson: FBI,* a two-hour movie based on her life, didn't make her a star among her peers. The movie marked the first time any FBI agent's life had been portrayed on national television.

Gibson has no answers for why such discrimination, however subtle, continues to exist. "There are just certain things they don't accept," she said. But neither will she deny the reality of her experiences. With some ten thousand agents in the bureau, she said, "the black female is the last person to be looked upon when it comes to promotions."

"I've fought that for a long time," she added. "There's no reason it should be this way."

And when times get tough, there's one thing Gibson can always count on to get her through: her faith in God. It is a faith she inherited when, as a child, she sat with her mother in the light of a kerosene lamp because the family couldn't afford electricity; in those quiet moments together, Gibson was taught that God never gives people more than they can bear. She still remembers her mother's words: "If ever there's a problem or anything you want in life, go to God, and if you *sincerely* ask Him for it, He will make a way for you to get it."

Gibson has operated her life on the belief "that God put me on earth to be someone of significance, a highly important black female." That has helped her handle obstacles such as divorce, being the single parent of a daughter with a lung condition, and even the stress of her profession. At times when her problems feel unbearable, Gibson finds peace in meditating and quietly reading the Bible. It gives her "a little strength to go on," she said. "I truly believe that there is a guardian angel watching over me and keeping me out of harm."

Her mother's counsel also has come in handy in her detective work. *"Listen,"* her mother always said. "You will learn *so* much." Thanks to that advice, Special Agent Gibson has learned how to size up a person in about five minutes. After a short conversation with a suspect, she can usually tell if the person is "a main player or if they're on the edge of it."

Once, after spending a little time with a man involved in a public corruption case, she realized that the suspect was "a low player" — but he had a lot of information she could use. So for three days, Gibson and her partner got as close to the fellow as they could. They wined and dined him, and made him believe that Gibson had a romantic interest in him. The ploy worked. The suspect spilled his guts, telling Gibson critical information that led to the arrest of a small-town Texas sheriff.

Gibson's savvy investigative work has even caught the attention of the elite Secret Service, which offered her a job. But this time, Gibson decided to stay put with the FBI. "Luckily," she said, "I just enjoy this job a whole lot better. The values I see in the FBI are a little bit different from those of the Secret Service."

A key responsibility of the Secret Service is to protect the President, a job that requires agents to "put their lives on the line," she said. While the FBI routinely faces similar dangers, it's different because agents are not focused on safeguarding an individual leader; they're concerned with "the protection of all," Gibson said.

Her job choice says a lot about this woman who's overcome seemingly insurmountable odds from the day she was born. Just like her employer, Special Agent Gibson is not one to set limits.

It's an approach that's served her well and one that she advocates for others who dream of success:

"Take the opportunity that is given. Run with it, use it extensively, sleep it, eat it, and grow wisely with it. Believe you are a very wonderful, talented individual and that you can be the President of the United States, if you so desire!"

Paula Giddings

★ | *Self-empowerment is about knowing who you are.*

For two generations in Paula Giddings's family, schools served as a sanctuary from the despair of being black in white America. Her family revered the value of education. They knew diplomas wouldn't stop the discrimination that shadowed their lives, but they believed a good education would give them economic security in their half of a segregated world.

"My maternal grandmother left rural Virginia during the World War I black migration years for Yonkers, New York, so that she could finish high school and earn enough as a domestic to send her daughter to college," Giddings said. "She was able to do so despite the Depression."

As a result, Giddings's mother became the first in her family to graduate from college. She eventually earned a master's degree while holding two jobs and caring for a child. Giddings's father also was college-educated. Her mother, Giddings said, "confesses that one of the things that attracted her to my dashing father was the fact that he was a college graduate from New York University, as his father was."

Giddings's paternal grandfather had taken full advantage of his education. He became the assistant city engineer for Yonkers, but was prevented from attaining the engineer's position because of his race. "Nevertheless," Giddings said, "he was a great believer in the idea that whites could be enlightened about blacks, and he worked toward that end in the civic affairs of the city and state."

Naturally, as a young girl Giddings possessed great expectations for her own education. But, as a child who came of age amid the racial turbulence of the sixties, she was sadly disappointed. Instead of enlightenment, Giddings encountered closed minds and racist attitudes among her teachers and classmates. For her, schools provided neither sanctuary nor security.

"In the sixties, when the crunch came, when the necessity arose for them to talk to us honestly about the issue of race, they proved themselves unworthy," she said. "I lost faith in them.

"My generation, especially those of us in the desegregating North," she said, "needed something other than financial security, deferred justice, or a compromised notion of 'quality of life' from our educations. As early as elementary school, I realized that what these institutions offered would fall woefully short in an era of racial ferment."

As an adult, pursuing a successful career as an editor and writer, Giddings never forgot the intellectual deprivation she felt as a black student. Instead, she drew on that experience to write groundbreaking books on racism and sexism in America, earning a reputation as a gifted writer and thinker. Today, ironically, that reputation has brought Giddings back to the place she studiously avoided for many years—the classroom. In 1989, she was appointed to a chair in women's studies at Douglass College, the women's college of Rutgers University. Subsequently, she taught at Spelman College in Atlanta and is now a Visiting Professor at Princeton University.

When Giddings returned to the classroom, it wasn't the first time she had been asked to teach. But she had spurned repeated offers because of her classroom experiences as a student. "During my twenty-year career as an editor and writer, I had actually gone out of my way to avoid institutions of higher education," she said.

When she was asked to teach at Douglas, Giddings began questioning the motivations that had kept her away from the classroom in her adult life. Accepting the offer, Giddings forced herself to come face-to-face with long-held perceptions about education in America. She had to ask herself: did today's classrooms offer students any more than what she had found? And, as a professor, could she meet her own students' expectations? In short, had the classroom changed at all?

"Certainly the movements have made them better places than they used to be," she said, explaining that racism and sexism are more

Paula Giddings   Photo: courtesy of Spelman College

openly discussed. And the progress of women's studies is an optimistic sign, although black feminist scholars continue to be frustrated, she said.

Giddings hopes that America's future holds a truly pluralistic society made up of different races and ethnic groups. During the last thirty years, Giddings feels, America has pulled apart the pieces of its racial puzzle, and it is now time to reassemble that puzzle in a way in which ideas of difference don't create such conflict. "A key to such reassessment is found in the academy," she said. "And if it is not to fail us once more, much of the work, I think, must be done by women and people of color."

It is a role Giddings has watched in the classroom before—played by her own mother.

Giddings first experienced racism in the classroom when her parents sent her to a private school. As the first African-American child to attend Halsted, she had problems from the start.

"One day, one of my schoolmates started calling me racial names. 'Coffeepot' was one, I remember, and the other students soon chimed in," she said.

As the racial slurs continued, school administrators realized they had a big problem. Unable to handle it, they called Giddings's mother for help. Lucky for them—and for Giddings—her mother was a teacher and guidance counselor.

"I remember her coming to the class and reading some book about 'difference,'" Giddings said. "After she read, my mother coaxed my classmates to air their stereotypical attitudes about blacks (which were hair-raising) and then firmly but gently corrected them."

After that, things became easier for Giddings in school. But the episode taught her a lesson that would influence the rest of her life.

"I learned very early that essential information about race—information that could resolve even the simplest problem, that could deepen knowledge and understanding—would have to come from outside of school. Today I realize why," Giddings later reflected in a 1990 essay called "Education, Race, and Reality: A Legacy of the '60s."

During the fifties and sixties, when Giddings was growing up, schools simply didn't have the right tools for dealing with racism. Textbooks painted the image of an America that was as pure as homogenized milk. There was little mention of ethnic or racial groups, much less of any tension between them.

"And the word 'racism' never formed on the lips," said Giddings.

She can remember only one reference to race, a brief mention of slavery in a history book: "What lingers in my mind is an illustration depicting three or four generations of a slave family in the 'quarters,' peering back at me with mouths that grinned, but eyes that were strangely expressionless."

During this period it was assumed that blacks would follow the path of European immigrants, who had blended into the great American melting pot. So when a little white boy threw racial slurs at a little black girl, schools simply weren't prepared to deal with it.

But then came the first dramatic stirrings of the civil rights movement: a group of idealists boarded buses and headed into the South to challenge racial segregation. Known as the Freedom Rides, the 1961 bus trips attracted both black and white protestors. At the time, Giddings was 13 and living in an all-white neighborhood.

"The Freedom Rides were the most transforming event of my childhood," Giddings said. "I would never think quite the same again, about myself, about my generation, about race in this country, about the value of education."

Giddings became enthralled with the riders, and anxiously followed the news of their travels through six states.

"I was filled with emotion," she said. "I felt so proud as I watched them board those buses; their faces, set with determination, gave me chills. And I shared their triumph when the buses got through the first states without incident."

Then the riders hit Anniston, Alabama, where mobs of angry whites waited with firebombs and tire irons. The next pictures Giddings saw portrayed bloodied riders. "What made people do this to people they didn't even know?" Giddings wondered at the time. "And where did the courage and the inspiration of the activists come from?"

Although her parents believed in self-esteem for their race, they had no answers to their daughter's troubling questions.

"Not because they didn't know," said Giddings. "My father founded the Yonkers chapter of the Congress of Racial Equality, which sponsored the rides—but they were afraid of discouraging you or making you too angry or hateful."

Even though the ground was shaking under Giddings, it remained remarkably still for those around her. The Freedom Rides were never mentioned at her school. And when she brought them up, all she got in return were blank stares — "it was as if I was talking about some strange and distant thing."

That's when Giddings began knitting together experiences and impressions that would turn her away from, if not against, educational institutions for many years. "I began to understand: if the institution could not deal with the encompassing notion of race, one also had to question the entire nature of reality as expressed in institutional life."

Giddings became convinced that racism was purposely overlooked when she saw how the schools handled other kinds of explosive events.

"When John Fitzgerald Kennedy was assassinated in 1963, the news was broadcast over the school loudspeaker," said Giddings. The principal offered a prayer, and students wept. In her English class, when they studied Shakespeare, her teacher gave an unforgettable lesson on the nature of tragedy.

But where were the lessons on racism?

When it was time for college, Giddings refused to attend another mostly white school. She chose the historically black Howard University, because she knew it would be a place "where race would be a subject of study — where I would find a context and community."

Although she enjoyed the atmosphere of a black school, Giddings was often disappointed in her courses. She was assigned to read American classics by authors who had defended segregation, without those ideas being challenged.

She began to realize that educational institutions didn't just overlook racial issues, they avoided them altogether. And nowhere was this more true than at black colleges, because their mission historically had been to train and socialize African-Americans to find jobs in the work force — "a work force that depended on stability and absence of strife," said Giddings.

Black colleges didn't want white society afraid that they were producing disgruntled thinkers who might scoff at becoming a drone — even a professional one. Or worse yet, spread discontent among other workers.

Giddings found the role of black women to be even more distressing. They were good enough to become teachers or enter other helping professions, but nothing more.

"Our education certainly wasn't designed to produce intellectuals or a life of the mind," she said. Black women at black schools were still expected to serve until they dropped, Giddings said.

Such feelings caused Giddings to abandon the world of academia after graduating from Howard in 1969. "To the disappointment of my family, I decided that I had had enough of educational institutions after Howard," she said.

Giddings decided to pursue a career in publishing as a book editor. She went to work for Random House in New York as an editorial secretary. A year later, she was promoted to copy editor.

In 1972, she moved to Howard University Press, where she worked for three years before venturing into journalism, writing for *Encore American* and *Worldwide News.* She was assigned to open a Paris office of the magazine, and had many opportunities to travel throughout Europe and to South Africa, Uganda, and Kenya for stories, and to interview prominent people such as Winnie Mandela.

She returned to the United States in 1977 and continued to write. During the course of her career, her work has appeared in numerous well-known publications, including *The New York Times* and *Essence.*

In 1979, she became part of a federally funded project on black women's history that eventually led to her two books—and convinced her that it's important for black women to know the contributions that other black women have made in the past.

In a ground-breaking book, *When and Where I Enter: The Impact of Black Women on Race and Sex in America,* Giddings explored the relationship of racism and sexism. Because both are fueled by people wanting to control power and wealth, it is only logical that those who want to undermine blacks also want to hold back women.

Black women understood they were being forced to fight both evils; most white women did not, Giddings concluded. White feminists often bowed to racism, and hurt their own cause in the process—because, like it or not, women's greatest gains have come in the wake of blacks' demands for rights.

Black women have been often forced to make difficult choices. "Women's rights were an empty promise if African-Americans were crushed under the heel of a racist power structure," said Giddings. "At the same time, it was important to act on the fact that sexism can be as devastating as racism."

When and Where I Enter, a project Giddings undertook with the support of a Ford Foundation grant, was published in 1984. Four years later, she produced her second book on the social and political history of African-American women, *In Search of Sisterhood: Delta Sigma Theta and the Challenge of the Black Sorority Movement.*

Even now, as she ventures into education as a professor of women's studies, Giddings has not forfeited her first love—writing. Currently, she is working on a biography of black American journalist Ida B. Wells.

"I will write till I say good-bye to this world," Giddings said.

Karl Hampton

★ *You've got to know who you are and where you came from, and feel strongly about that. Nothing is impossible if you believe in yourself and believe you can achieve whatever you wish.*

Karl Hampton's father never wanted his son to grow up like him. That's why, season after season, as they toiled in the cotton fields of Mississippi, the father cautioned his only son: "If you get an education, you won't have to do this type of hard labor to make a living."

Valuing his father's counsel and his rural roots has enabled Hampton to build a successful career that blends both influences. At 31, he is an agricultural economist with the Foreign Agricultural Service of the U.S. Department of Agriculture. His job involves removing foreign barriers to U.S. agricultural products and helping to set policy on issues of international trade. These responsibilities have taken Hampton to foreign countries ranging from France to India. Currently, he's on a three-year assignment in Brazil as an assistant agricultural attaché.

That's a far cry from Isola, Mississippi, the country crossroads where Hampton's family farms some seven hundred acres of soybeans and cotton. Helping his father in the fields gave the young Hampton "the motivation to want the best out of life," he said.

"Don't get me wrong—the cotton fields of Mississippi taught me a lot about life. I am proud of that foundation and have no wish to change it."

But Hampton also candidly acknowledges the impact a rural upbringing has had on his life. "The connotation attached to a black man from Mississippi does not open any doors of opportunity for you," he said. "I found I had to prove myself endlessly in terms of intelligence, ambition, and adaptability."

Ambition is something Hampton seems to have by the bushel. Even as a boy, he was painfully aware that rural Isola was a cultural backwash and felt that he was "isolated from everything." Though he has come to appreciate how much he learned from the solid, simple folk who filled his childhood, at the time he hungered for more worldly company.

"If I could add one thing to my life, it would have been the presence of more experienced and influential people to surround me," he said. "People to guide me to a higher plateau. Growing up, I would have benefited from someone who was exposed to various places and situations — someone who could have broadened my narrow perspective fostered by living on a farm in a small town."

But what he did have was the loving encouragement of parents who were determined that all six of their kids would go to college. "That was really an accomplishment since our father never finished school. My mother did — but neither of them ever went to college," Hampton said.

His parents realized their dreams. Hampton and his five sisters are all successful professionals with impressive careers — one is a computer expert, for example, another a doctor, and another a teacher.

"My parents were the reason for us turning out like we did," he said. "I think if it weren't for them I wouldn't be where I am today."

Teachers also played an important role in Hampton's life. He can still recall the words of his high school math teacher, who "would always tell me to never play myself cheap," Hampton said. "I felt she saw something in me and she wanted me to do the very best I could — to not settle for anything less than what I was capable of doing, or what I was capable of being."

A disciplined youth, Hampton excelled academically and athletically — and he capitalized on both abilities to build his future.

As a teenager, Hampton rode the school bus fourteen miles round trip to Belzoni, where he attended middle school and high school, along with every other kid in the county. A big kid for his age, Hampton began playing football in junior high. In high school, he became a local star on the football field and basketball court.

Among the one hundred kids in his graduating class, Hampton was a top student — he missed becoming valedictorian by a couple of grade points. But he was offered a full academic and

Karl Hampton

athletic scholarship to Alcorn State University in Lorman, Mississippi.

Hampton approached college in 1980 with a sense of wonder tempered by his father's wisdom. Determined that his life would be guided by his brains, not his brawn, Hampton decided to "use sports to get a free education." As much as he loved playing football, he always thought of himself as a student first, an athlete second.

But his athletic activities could have easily overshadowed his academic ambitions. In spite of the amount of time required to practice and play college sports, Hampton said, "I was determined to graduate in four years—and nobody thought that it would be possible."

Academic expectations for athletes were often low, and Hampton came face-to-face with that stereotype the first day of his freshman chemistry class.

"Wait a minute," the professor said as he entered the classroom. "Are you a football player?"

"Yes, ma'am," Hampton answered.

"Then you might as well turn around and walk out that door right now," the professor said, "because you're going to flunk my class."

"Excuse me," Hampton said. "You don't even know me, and you tell me I'm going to flunk your class."

At that moment, Hampton made up his mind that he wasn't just going to pass chemistry—he was going to ace the course.

"I got an *A* on every test she gave," he recalled. "After that, every time a football player would come into her class, she would tell them, 'If you don't know Karl Hampton, you should find out who he is and get to know him because that's a young man everybody needs to know.'

"I think I kind of changed her opinion about football players," he said with a smile.

Hampton also made a reputation for himself on the football field. He finished sixth on Alcorn's all-time football receiving list, and helped his team, the Alcorn State Braves, to an undefeated season and a place in the playoffs in 1985.

College, especially traveling to away games with the team, gave Hampton his first, long-awaited glimpse of life beyond Isola. "I never really got a chance to go anyplace until I went to college and started playing ball," he said.

Altogether, Hampton reaped five years of education from his scholarship. In characteristic fashion, he decided to take advantage of the fact that, although he had gone out for the football team his freshman year, he hadn't played. That meant he was eligible to play one more year after graduating with his bachelor's degree in agricultural education. And that meant he could get a master's degree—because as long as he was playing, the college was paying.

In 1987, with only nine hours left on his second degree, Hampton was offered a job as an assistant county agent with the Mississippi Cooperative Extension Service. While working, he continued his education, earning a master's degree in agricultural economics in 1987.

His work as a Greenville County extension agent returned Hampton to the farm—this time in the role of teacher. At least two or three days a week he would visit local farmers to educate them on the latest developments in agricultural research and demonstrate new technology and equipment, and better ways to work the land.

Hampton had been working as an extension agent for about a year and a half when the impact of the Reagan years hit rural Mississippi. Facing the possibility of budget cuts in the extension agency, as well as some realizations about his own ambitions, Hampton knew it was time for a change: "The job I was in was probably one of the better jobs in the state of Mississippi, but I knew I wanted more out of life than being there."

He updated his résumé and mailed about forty to various companies and government agencies. Though response was good, there were no jobs to be had; many of the places where he applied were strapped with hiring freezes.

Finding his job in Washington was a matter of luck and timing, Hampton said. "I had one résumé left," he said, when he happened across an ad for the USDA Foreign Agriculture Service while thumbing through a friend's magazine. At the time, he thought, "Well, this is a long shot, but what do I have to lose."

Nothing, it turned out. A week later, he got a call inviting him to come to Washington for an interview.

In some ways, what Hampton does now is not so very different from the work he did as a county agent—except he's dealing with whole countries. And that's a critical difference, because it means Hampton is routinely exposed to new environments and foreign cultures. He's even learned another language: to prepare for his Brazil assignment, Hampton took a crash course in Portuguese.

Back home, his adventures have made him a local celebrity of sorts. "The people down in Mississippi are totally excited," he said. "But I'm still the same person, and as always, my goals keep getting higher."

Sometimes those goals are just for fun—like winning the contest that put him on national TV in his underwear.

In June 1991, Hampton and a friend became intrigued by a contest ad in *Cosmopolitan* magazine. The Jockey underwear company was looking for "real people" to model their products for a national advertising campaign.

It was an opportunity Hampton couldn't pass by. He figured a pair of boxer shorts would hang rather nicely on his six-foot-three athletic frame, so while he modeled, his friend snapped a photo.

In addition, Jockey wanted contest applicants to write twenty-five-word essays describing why they should be the ones to represent the company. In typical fashion, Hampton wasn't content to rely on his physique.

He already knew a little bit about Jockey, since the company has a manufacturing plant in his hometown. So he went to the library and "really researched the industry," to make sure his essay showed an understanding of the company's goals, he said.

The extra effort paid off. Three thousand people entered the Jockey competition, and Hampton stayed in the running through several cuts to narrow the field of contestants. The final competition was an interview with a company vice president. Hampton passed that test, too, with flying colors and was named one of six finalists.

He was invited to appear on the *Live with Regis and Kathy Lee* show in November for the announcement of the winner. The show set up its stage so that each of the six finalists was presented in a typical underwear scene—Hampton was in his shorts at an ironing board, ironing a shirt as if he were getting ready to go to work.

Before the show went on the air, the finalists were coached: act surprised, like on the Miss America Pageant. So when Hampton heard his name called out as the *winner,* he played his part to perfection, clapping his hands to his cheeks, his mouth flying open as if to say "oh my"—much to the delight of the studio audience.

That was the beginning of Hampton's brief flirtation with fame. The contest was covered on *Entertainment Tonight* and by the Black Entertainment Network. But perhaps the thing that tickled Hampton the most was having David Letterman joke about him on *Late Night with David Letterman.*

In March, the ad campaign that had inspired the contest appeared in magazines across the country. Sporting Jockey shorts, Hampton was pictured in such prestigious publications as *The New York Times Magazine.*

All in all, the contest was great fun, Hampton said. And who knows, maybe something will come of it—like an invitation to do a commercial, or maybe even a TV show.

One thing is certain. If there's an opportunity in there somewhere,

Hampton will find it, and make the most of it. That's just the way he is, thanks to an upbringing which encouraged his ambitions early and endowed him with the self-confidence to believe that, with hard work, he can make his dreams come true.

"I know who I am, and what I am capable of achieving," he said. "I have been tested many times, but my belief in my own abilities has guided me through.

"My confidence helps me set goals and work toward them. Nothing is impossible if you believe in yourself and believe you can achieve whatever you wish," he said.

Since taking the job in Washington, Hampton has made several trips back to Mississippi, and his alma mater, to talk with young people about his work and to share the lessons that have guided his life. It's his way of repaying all the folks who contributed to the success he now enjoys.

"I can remember everyone who ever did something for me," he said. "And now I want to reach back and give others a hand."

Hampton encourages young people to take advantage of every opportunity that's given to them.

"Excel to your utmost, so you never have to say 'I could have done more, I could have done it better.' "

Yvonne Jackson

 Know who you are and what you value and then find the places in life where those connect.

As a vice president of human resources for a Fortune 500 company, Yvonne Jackson has a front row seat for what experts predict will be one of the most important trends in the twenty-first century: the changing face of America.

Minorities, immigrants, and women are expected to make up 80 percent of the people entering the work force between 1985 and the year 2000. Already many companies, including Jackson's employer, Avon Products, are looking for ways to create opportunities for this diverse work force.

As a black professional woman, Jackson, 43, has personally encountered the racist and sexist biases that employers expect to grapple with as the work force changes. She routinely puts those experiences to work in her job. As head of the department that develops personnel policy and procedures for Avon's 7,400 U.S. employees, Jackson plays a pivotal role in determining how the company treats its people.

Avon understands that work force diversity and the company's bottom line are linked. "We reach millions of women a year through direct sales," Jackson said. "As a consumer-oriented beauty company operating in over one hundred countries, our multicultural and predominantly female customer base expects us to be a company that hires and promotes minorities and women.

"For us, managing diversity throughout all levels of the company—from senior management on down—just makes good business sense," she said.

Good business sense is something Jackson has possessed since she was a young girl growing up in Los Angeles, California. Her enterprising spirit surfaced in fifth grade after she received a hand loom at Christmas. Before long, she was peddling potholders to neighbors and friends.

At 13, she went out and got herself a job with a neighborhood cleaners because she wanted to make her own money. Her parents encouraged that sense of responsibility: one rule Jackson remembers from her childhood was that she was expected to earn enough money to make the down payment on her college tuition each year.

That meant working three jobs one summer when she wanted to go to Colorado to be in a friend's wedding before returning to school. "My mother said that's fine, I'll even buy your dress for you—but are you going to have your money for college?" Jackson recalled with a smile.

One of four daughters, Jackson has an identical twin sister, Yvette, whom she's always been very close to. They grew up in Watts, a neighborhood that provided a strong sense of community. By her own account, Jackson's childhood, though ordinary by most middle-class standards, was more comfortable than many blacks enjoyed at that time. "We all went to the same church, and we all belonged to the Girl Scouts, and did all the things that all other kids do," she said.

But beyond the boundaries of that community and her all-American family, life was more complex. Attending public schools, Jackson was exposed to the harsher realities of urban life. "There were drug dealers, and all kinds of stuff going on around me," Jackson said.

"There were bright, alert kids on their way to college, like my sisters and I. And then there were kids who were so disadvantaged they had basically shut down, and they were so ill-prepared for the world at large.

"I didn't know what to make of it," she said. "And I was too young then to understand the issues of depression and hopelessness that I see in black kids today."

The Jackson children had the benefit of growing up surrounded by positive role models, for their family had a long tradition of education and professional achievement. Jackson's father is a retired judge and a third-generation lawyer; his father—her grandfather—was an attorney and an active politician; and her great-grandfather was the first black attorney in Virginia.

On her mother's side it's a similar story. Her mother is college-educated, "as was her mother, as was her mother, as was her mother," Jackson said. They each chose teaching as a career because, historically, black women "had two choices in life," Jackson said. "You either cleaned other people's houses or you became a teacher."

As a young girl, Jackson was encouraged to continue that teaching tradition. But when it came time for her to pick a college and a profession, neither she nor her twin was drawn to an academic career. Intent on pursuing a business degree, Jackson headed to Atlanta, Georgia, to attend Spelman College.

It was a journey that would change her life.

Growing up in in L.A. hadn't prepared Jackson for the segregated South. She remembers her mother cautioning, "When you get there, make sure you get in a 'black' cab—go with a black cab driver." At the time, Jackson wondered, "Why would she tell me that? But I did it. Because I was 17, and it was my first time away from home, my first time away from my twin sister—ever, in my whole life."

Nor was the impressionable young Jackson prepared for the impact that Spelman, the nation's oldest all-black women's college, would have on her. "I remember going to chapel," she said, "and there were all these black women in one place—women who were attractive, and bright, and energized."

And when their voices joined in song, Jackson was hit by a wave of emotion that even today makes her eyes grow misty. "I remember tears going down my face, and thinking, 'How wonderful this is.' Here I was, surrounded by people like me, people who I could bond with immediately, and yet who were different from me, too."

Spelman encouraged her young spirit to soar while giving her a solid foundation for adulthood. "I was experimenting with life in a cocoon of comfort," Jackson said.

That sense was confirmed some years later when a Los Angeles psychologist studying twins talked with Jackson and her sister. What he discovered was a noticeable difference between Jackson, who had gone to a black women's college, and her twin, who had attended a white women's college in California. "There was a certain settledness and confidence about my experience that she didn't have—even at another women's college, in an environment very similar to Spelman," Jackson said. "So I think that Spel-

115

Yvonne Jackson

man was very profound in building my confidence level, and in helping me develop at that age in my life—which I'm sure has served me well."

After graduating from Spelman in 1970 with a degree in history and business administration, Jackson went to work for Sears, Roebuck & Co. After receiving training to be a division manager, she was put in charge of the toy department in the Sears store in Torrance, California.

"That was my first experience in being the 'first of,' " she said. Until Jackson was hired, Sears had no black females running departments in the Los Angeles region.

"I was naive," she recalled. "I'd come out of this warm Spelman cocoon, and I didn't think much about the world into which I was launching myself and how other people might perceive me—not because of my abilities but because of who I was. And I began to realize that I was dealing with another dynamic."

Bright, energetic, enterprising Jackson was forced to see herself through the eyes of people who didn't know her and certainly weren't inclined to believe the best about her.

"The perceptions other people have are sometimes a deficit," Jackson said. "They look at me and they see a black woman, and they assume, number one, that she's incompetent—why is she here? And so there are certain assumptions that come with people thinking that way, and which I'm working against.

"That didn't hit me at first, but it became a learned reality over time." She remembers how other employees reacted when she arrived at her first store. She was bombarded with questions such as: "Where'd you come from?" and "What's your educational background?" and "What gives you the right to be here?" and "How come you're telling us what to do?"

Her naiveté soon gave way to the sad realization that such questions were part of the bargain of being a black professional woman. And while improved race relations have discouraged people from asking those questions as directly as her first employees did, Jackson doesn't kid herself that she and others like her aren't constantly being put to the test.

"It took me a long while to figure that out," Jackson said. "I became aware that I had to prove myself upon impact—that I had to say and do things to get people comfortable so that they could relax and realize I was a normal human being, just like they were. I had a mother, a father, and sisters. I was trying to buy a car and do all the same things they were trying to do in their lives.

"I had to make them realize I was a person—not somebody who had just dropped down from Mars, but a human being who had feelings and emotions. And frankly, I think that's been one of the things that have gotten me through in all the different levels of jobs I've held—that I can make people comfortable."

But with equal candor, Jackson admitted, "It's cost me a lot, too. Because I realize there are times I've made people so comfortable that they don't think of me as black."

In particular, she remembers one Avon executive who told her more than once when they were working together, "Yvonne, I don't see you as black."

Her response: "But I am. I am very black."

Because the two had a close and positive working relationship, Jackson realized what he was saying "was a compliment in some ways, but it was also painful. I remember being hurt by that, really deeply hurt."

That was several years ago. But even now, Jackson finds it hard to talk about it. Even more difficult is putting into words the complex thoughts and feelings she has about combining her black heritage and her womanhood with a successful career in mainstream American business.

Jackson's worked at Avon headquarters in New York City since 1979. She was attracted to the company's "caring spirit" and its focus on meeting the needs of women, in terms of both products and earnings opportunities.

Recalling her job interviews and her first impressions of Avon, Jackson said, "There was just something about it I liked. It felt comfortable and free—and I thought it would be a good place to be."

Joining the company as an executive recruiter in human resources, Jackson has held a succession of increasingly responsible jobs over the past fourteen years. At one point in her career, during the late eighties, she traveled extensively to Japan, the United Kingdom, Brazil, and Mexico as part of her responsibilities for international human resources.

That she would choose to build her career at Avon, which has earned a reputation as a "women's company," comes as no surprise. Most of the important lessons in Jackson's life have occurred in the company of women.

Some of her happiest childhood memories feature her grandmother, a no-nonsense woman who led a cosmopolitan existence in Ardmore, Oklahoma.

"My grandmother was a woman way before her time," Jackson

said. "She didn't marry till she was 30 years old because she had to do things—she had to educate herself, she had to travel places, and even as she had six kids but no money, she continued to educate herself."

Though her grandfather never left Ardmore until he was 80 and illness forced him to relocate to a warmer climate, Jackson's grandmother was a woman who knew no limits.

"She went one summer—I'll never forget this story because I know it's the roundabout way I got to Spelman—with her two youngest kids to study education at Atlanta University on a graduate basis. And they all stayed in the dormitory together," Jackson said. Another time, with kids in tow, she traveled to New York to study millinery because she wanted to teach it in her home economics classes.

"That was my grandmother—she just kept trying to make herself better."

Until she was 13, Jackson spent every summer with her grandparents; at one point, she and her twin sister moved to Oklahoma for about a year while their parents went through a divorce.

Jackson wouldn't trade those times with her grandmother for anything. "I learned so much from her during those summers and that year."

Often after school, the twins would be given an hour's worth of geography lessons from their grandmother. "We knew everything on that globe—every country, every capital of every country," Jackson said. "I mean, she'd say how many Christmas Islands are there?"

And Jackson would be expected to name them. "You probably don't realize this," she said, "but there are twenty-three islands in this world that are called Christmas.

"Those are the kinds of things my grandmother knew. She gave of herself in terms of teaching us, in terms of disciplining us. I call that caring about kids' growth—because you just always felt the love that was there."

Her grandmother's teachings have stayed with Jackson. "I think I developed discipline as a result of my experiences with her, but also worldliness—worldliness in the sense that the world is big, that it isn't just Ardmore, Oklahoma, or Los Angeles, California," Jackson said.

Her grandmother's thirst for knowledge and drive for a better life are values that have been passed from generation to generation, for as long as anyone in the family can remember. "They were all about doing something more, doing something better, not simply accepting the fact that they were black, in a segregated environment," Jackson said. "They wanted to be the best, to be good at what they did."

Now Jackson is living those words. The values she was taught as a child and her own experiences in building a career have shaped her into a successful professional woman who cares deeply about people. And that concern goes beyond the demands of her job.

For many years, Jackson shared her expertise in managing people by teaching a class at the Fashion Institute of Technology in New York City. She's active in the community, serving on the board of the Northside Center for Child Development and working with the Harlem YMCA's Black Achievers program. Spelman is still very much a part of her life: she serves on their Corporate Women's Roundtable and regularly returns to the campus to talk with students about her work and the world that awaits them.

"And I see the faces of these hundreds of college women and I am just so proud of them because they're so bright and they just need that nurturing so they can go out and do it—do what they do well."

The same might be said of America's changing work force—the minorities, immigrants, and women who will come to corporations like Avon in search of the opportunities to prove their worth. Though Jackson is low-key about the executive status she has achieved, the fact is, she will be a powerful voice in determining how Avon welcomes this diverse work force.

Hard work, clear-headed determination, and a keen sense of social responsibility have propelled Jackson to the top of her profession. The day-to-day demands of her job can be rigorous—and it's not unusual for the company president to call her on a Saturday to talk business.

When he does, Jackson's likely as not to be curled up on her couch, reading a favorite book, or puttering around her country home with her husband. But that's a relatively new achievement for Jackson, who's decided her definition of success is "balance."

Striking a balance between a successful career and a satisfying personal life does not come easily to Jackson, who describes herself as a workaholic.

"I can work hours upon hours, if I have to," she said. "I've learned over the past few years to try to balance that a little bit more. But I don't always do it very well."

Achieving balance is a matter of understanding what's important — truly important — to you, said Jackson, who offers this advice to young people:

"It probably sounds trite," she said, "but be yourself.

"Know who you are and what you value, and then find the places in life where those connect. It's not always easy, and sometimes it can't be satisfied in any one place. But to have a good life, you must be determined to find that fit."

Quincy Jones

★ | *I had such a thirsty mind. I wanted to learn everything . . . I've always believed that you need to learn everything you can about your field and try to be the best.*

Prolific. Versatile. Genius. The reigning master. After more than forty years in show business, music man Quincy Jones has had almost every adjective and accolade imaginable linked with his name.

He's more than earned the adoration—his music was even the first played on the moon. Astronaut Buzz Aldrin tells the story that just as he was getting ready to step off the spacecraft, he reached back for a cassette of "Fly Me to the Moon"—a song Jones had arranged and conducted for Count Basie and Frank Sinatra—to accompany his first lunar stroll.

Jones has lived a diverse and storybook career. When he began playing trumpet professionally as a teenager, audiences were still swinging to Basie, not rocking to Elvis.

Today, approaching age 60, Jones regularly puts in twelve- to fourteen-hour days and remains acutely attuned to the latest musical styles and trends. Trumpeter, composer, arranger, producer—the maestro has left no musical stone unturned. He can still swing to a jazz beat, but Jones also knows how to rock and rap.

Jones's career credits read like a who's who of the superstars, hit songs, and famed musical styles of the past four decades. At age 15, he was playing in a band with the now legendary Ray Charles. At age 18, he was touring with jazz great Lionel Hampton. Among the other stars for whom Jones has arranged, composed and produced: Billie Holiday, Count Basie, Duke Ellington, Sammy Davis, Jr., Sarah Vaughn, Dizzy Gillespie, Frank Sinatra, George Benson, Chaka Kahn, and Michael Jackson.

He's scored music for more than three dozen films, including *The Wiz, In Cold Blood, In the Heat of the Night,* and *Roots*—as well as *The Color Purple;* the 1986 movie was the first Jones also co-produced. And he's recorded numerous albums of his own, including his 1990 hit "Back on the Block," which has sold more than three million copies.

As a producer, Jones helped Michael Jackson achieve stratospheric superstar status with "Thriller," the best-selling album of all time. More than forty-one million copies have been sold. He also produced "We Are the World," the best-selling single in the 1980s that featured an all-star musical cast to help raise relief funds for famine victims in Africa. More than four million copies were sold.

Along the way, Jones has accumulated numerous distinctions and awards. In 1964, he was hired as a vice president at Mercury Records—the first black to hold such a position at a white-owned record company.

He has been nominated for seventy-six Grammy awards and won twenty-five. His album "The Dude" earned an unprecedented twelve Grammy nominations in 1981 and won five. In 1983, he received eight Grammy awards, the most ever by one person in a single year. He followed that up in 1984 with several more Grammys, including one for Producer of the Year for Michael Jackson's "Thriller" album. Then in 1990, he earned another six Grammys for "Back on the Block." In the movie category, Jones has received four Oscar nominations for his film scores.

The awards and credits pay tribute to a man with a deep reservoir of talent. But Jones's prestigious bio also implies an effortlessness that belies how fortunate he's been at critical junctures in his life, how hard he's worked for his accomplishments, and how far he's traveled since childhood to reach the pinnacle of his profession.

When Jones was born in 1933, his family lived in Chicago's rough, impoverished South Side. Life was precarious, and there were no role models for black kids living in an inner-city ghetto.

"Think of it," Jones said. "There was no TV. The only black on radio was Rochester. Even Amos and Andy were white. In sports, there was Joe Louis. How can anybody grow up and aspire to something if it doesn't exist?"

Tragedy split Jones's family apart when he was 8. His mother, who

Quincy Jones   Photo: Greg Gorman

Jones said could speak seven languages, had to be committed to a
state mental institution. His father, a skilled carpenter, remarried two
years later and moved the family to the West Coast because he
couldn't find work in Chicago.

Later in life, Jones learned from a doctor that his mother's mental
problems could have been cured with vitamins. "I didn't know
where she went," he said, "and for ten years I never saw her again."

In Bremerton, Washington, near Seattle, Jones's father found less racism than in Chicago and more opportunity. Jobs in area shipyards were plentiful, so he settled the family there.

It was a fortuitous move for Jones. The local music scene was very active, and Jones began hanging out with such jazz musicians as Duke Ellington and Billy Eckstine when they came through the Seattle area. Jones also soon met a young Ray Charles, who first got him interested in composing music.

"Ray, he opened my eyes to orchestration," Jones said. "I was trying to unlock that magical door to what orchestration was all about. How do you get eight trombones and eight trumpets playing the same song? And he explained how you key them. I had such a thirsty mind, I wanted to learn everything."

Jones soon formed a band with Charles, and his musical career was on its way. Word traveled quickly through the jazz world that Jones was a natural talent, and he began playing with a variety of musicians.

Jones's talent and reputation earned him a scholarship to the Berklee College of Music in Boston. After graduating from Berklee, Jones toured as a trumpeter with Dizzy Gillespie, then formed his own large band for tours in America and Europe.

Today, Jones has the professional freedom to work on whatever interests him. He has his own record label, Qwest, and actively pursues new talent. He nurtures young performers, especially black ones.

In 1990, he signed a joint partnership deal with Time Warner Enterprises, a division of Time Warner Inc., to form Quincy Jones Entertainment Company. The deal allows Jones to produce television shows and movies, among other things. The hit TV sitcom *Fresh Prince of Bel Air* was one of his first projects. Time Publishing Ventures and Quincy Jones Entertainment also have teamed up to publish *Vibe,* a magazine focused on the rap-influenced culture of hip-hop.

Jones's influence spreads far and wide.

"I don't know how he ever gets any work done," said Kimiko Jackson, the director of feature films for Quincy Jones Entertainment. "I'll be up at the house with him and it's unbelievable. Marlon Brando calls. Or Michael Jackson. Then it's Henry Mancini or Jesse Jackson. I just sit there with my mouth open."

Established performers relish the chance to work with Jones. As a producer, he is known for bringing out the best in a musician or singer. "You want to please him, you want to impress him," said performer Barbra Streisand.

Said singer-songwriter Paul Simon: "I don't know anybody with the musical credibility of Quincy. He has a tremendous overview of music. He knows history. He knows his players."

Jones's hectic and demanding professional life has taken its toll on his personal life. His three marriages have ended in divorce, and his six children didn't get to spend much time with their famous father when they were kids.

But these days Jones strives to maintain a balance. He began to rethink his life after two blood vessels ruptured in his brain in 1975, nearly killing him and requiring two operations to repair. "I know it's a cliché, but my whole life really did pass in front of me," he said. "And I thought, I never did tell so-and-so how I felt, and I never answered that letter. So I started putting my mouth where my heart was."

After recovering from surgery, Jones began practicing Hatha-Yoga, which consists of various exercises that strengthen the body and mind. He also began re-establishing ties with his children.

"It's not that I'm working less," he said of his new, balanced lifestyle, "but I'm trying to play more."

But one thing hasn't changed and probably never will—Jones's drive to reach new heights: "I haven't even touched the surface of all the things I want to do. There are always new challenges to tackle."

Brady Keys, Jr.

★ | *With me, you get a chance to make a real*
difference. You get a chance to make a statement.

Brady Keys, Jr., grew up dirt poor during the 1940s, barely surviving with only his mother in Austin, Texas. They were too poor for new shoes, too poor for regular meals. About the only thing his mother could afford to give her son was dreams. And that she did. The day her eight-year-old boy came to her and told his mama he dreamed of becoming a professional football player and successful business-man, she didn't hesitate in her encouragement. "Yes," she replied. "Yes, you can. Yes, you will."

Recalling the memory, Keys said, "From that moment on, I was pointed in the direction of success."

Almost fifty years later Keys has lived a life of dreams come true—for himself and countless others he has befriended along the way. Brady Keys, Jr., did indeed become a star professional football player, as well as a self-made millionaire businessman with a Midas touch for making money.

But the journey from little-boy dreams to adult success has been a long one for Keys, one filled with twists and turns, detours and dead ends. Looking back, Keys said, "The greatest personal obstacle in my career was my tremendous ability to get off track and chase women at a very young age. I just didn't feel that much else was important at a time when I had everything available to me."

As a teenager, Keys experienced the intoxicating attention that accompanies athletic stardom. He was blessed with a natural ability to handle a football, and made the varsity football team in both junior high and high school. When his mother married while he was still in high school and moved the family to Los Angeles, California, Keys got involved in other sports, too.

127

By the time his graduation rolled around, Keys had caught the attention of recruiters from several colleges. He even had an offer from a major league baseball club, the Brooklyn Dodgers.

In those days, he said, "they wouldn't let you play two sports." Forced to choose, Keys decided, "I didn't like baseball."

Keys had his eye on the future: he wanted to go to college. So he was drawn to an offer that included a scholarship from the University of California at Los Angeles. But his high school grades weren't scholarship material, and he ended up at a local junior college.

He discovered that his natural ability on the football field didn't apply to the classroom. His grades didn't cut it, so he dropped out of college and began playing semi-pro football.

A couple of years later, Keys got a second chance at a college education, when a scout from the Pittsburgh Steelers spotted him playing semi-pro ball and realized his potential. The scout promised to help Keys attend college until he could be legally drafted into the National Football League. During this time, he met and married Anna, who's been his wife ever since.

Keys entered Colorado State University. This time around, he knuckled down to his studies, working hard to get better grades. He also excelled at college football. By his third year, he qualified for the pros. "The Steelers sent me to CSU and then they pulled me out," Keys said.

For the next six years Keys played defensive halfback with the Steelers. He became an All-Pro on a Steelers defense that routinely finished first or second in its category.

His pro football dream realized, Keys turned his sights on his other ambition — to be a businessman. In 1967, with unprecedented financial backing from the Steelers, he started his first fast-food restaurant in San Diego, California. He christened it All-Pro Chicken.

Although things seemed to be going his way, Keys began having disagreements with Pittsburgh's management that led to his being traded to the Minnesota Vikings. He played for them for a year. Then, after a short stint with the St. Louis Cardinals, Keys left the NFL altogether — he said he is fairly certain he was being blackballed by team owners who were uncomfortable with his burgeoning success as a business owner.

But Keys had no intention of becoming a quitter. Faced with a challenge, Keys always relied upon his religious faith to see him through: "God has just blessed me, and blessed me, and blessed me. And forgiven me, and put me on the right track," he said. "Each time I lose something, He gives me more than I had before."

Based on his own experiences, Keys encourages teens and young adults to "seek God for your answers and guidance."

With religion as his compass, Keys went full steam ahead into the business world. Back in San Diego, he ran his restaurant with the help of his mother-in-law, her two sons, and his wife. It was such a success that within three months, he opened a second restaurant in San Diego, and then a third in Pittsburgh. That restaurant became the cornerstone of his franchise. Suddenly, it seemed, All-Pro Chicken was popping up all across the country.

After several profitable years in business, Keys made another major move in 1970: he bought a Burger King in Detroit's inner city. Just as he had with All-Pro, Keys grew the business, buying and building more Burger Kings until he became one of the largest employers of young people in Michigan. He also became the first black in the country to become a major franchiser of fast-food restaurants.

Just as important, he developed a reputation for being one of the best, achieving an employee retention rate that became the envy of his industry. "I don't lose people," he said. "With me you get a chance to make a real difference. You get a chance to make a statement."

Bigger businesses recognized that Keys was powerful competition and wanted to cash in on his success. In 1971, he struck a deal with Kentucky Fried Chicken to merge his All-Pro chain with their business. In the early eighties, Kentucky Fried Chicken made him an offer that sent him to Albany, Georgia, where he now lives. "I just couldn't turn that one down," he said.

Today, restaurants are only a portion of Keys's business interests. Through a series of deals in 1990, he sold all his Burger Kings, and he's cut back to only eleven Kentucky Fried Chicken restaurants.

Success has been a mixed blessing for Keys, though. Between his football talent and his business acumen, achieving wealth unusual for a black man in the sixties and seventies, Keys often has been thrust into public view. He's been criticized, scrutinized, and ostra-

Brady Keys, Jr.

cized more times than he cares to remember during the past three decades.

By many measures, Keys is a man of contrasts and contradictions. He defies stereotypes held by whites and blacks. A private man who believes a person should be measured by his deeds, he avoids confrontation, but he can't seem to escape controversy. He's regarded as a compassionate, generous man by those who know him personally; publically, he's been subjected to considerable scrutiny—often tinged with racism—by people who question his motives and seem to watch his every move as he goes about his business.

"Being Brady Keys is very difficult in this town," he once told a reporter for *The Albany Herald.* "There's always a story going around about me. I'm extremely misunderstood."

Take the time he decided to buy a house in the suburbs. He struck a deal, never dreaming his new home included a bonus: a racial tug-of-war.

But in no time, townsfolk were talking. Rumor had it Keys was working on a plan to infiltrate—and therefore integrate—the suburb's all-white country club. White business associates tried to talk him out of moving. Blacks in the community pushed him to put up a fight.

In the end, when his boxes were packed and moving trucks were backing into his new driveway, Keys was forced to face a hard truth: no matter whether he moved or stayed put, he'd made a lot of people angry.

"All I wanted was a house to live in," he said. "I really didn't want a fight."

But in one way or another, he's been battling discrimination most of his life.

For instance, some blacks in Arbor Hill, the "Little Harlem" part of his town, have faulted Keys for not using his power, money, and influence to fight against the city's undercurrent of racism. Other blacks, Keys said, assume that he's become too big "to relate to the little people."

White society, on the other hand, has seemed to accept him because of his wealth and business success. But the acceptance is tenuous at best.

Keys recalled an incident from his early days in Albany. He was in his restaurant, doing some paperwork, when a white couple walked in. Spotting Keys at his desk, they called him an "uppity nigger," loudly enough for all to hear, suggesting that he had no business "sitting there acting like he owns something."

Keys has never been one to waste time or energy challenging his critics or defending his position. "I never strike back when people

131

accuse me falsely," he said. Rather than confront the couple—and point out that he owned not only the very restaurant they were about to eat in, but several others—he decided it was time to work on his image. "I started portraying myself as a professional football player and sponsoring more community events."

Still, racism has continued to haunt Keys.

In 1991, when he bought WJIZ-FM, a local radio station that happened to be both Albany's largest and only black station, the volume of rumors about him increased. Folks speculated that he wanted to control the media so he could become mayor. Some even considered him dangerous after he added editorials and talk shows to the station's regular format of music and news.

As mysterious as Keys's motives may at times seem to the general public, close friends and business associates describe him as a genuine and unusually generous man who goes out of his way to help people. It's ironic, they say, that Keys seems to invite speculation precisely because he avoids publicity for his good deeds.

John Draper, a long-time friend and business associate, described Keys as "very human. You need that in business, where people are often very cold," Draper said. "There are not too many successful entrepreneurs like that. Black or white."

Draper believes Keys has succeeded because "he's like that motto for that California-brand wine: 'We sell no wine before its time.'

"He does things the good, old-fashioned way," Draper said. "He's an American hero because he's *worked* at it."

Keys said, "The single most important quality that led to my success is my absolute perseverance. I just will not give up, regardless of what it is. The second thing is focus."

Throughout his career, Keys has earned a reputation as a man who enjoys taking a chance on those who seem to have no chance at all. He's been known to hire people just out of jail or who have overcome drug addictions. A father of six, he loves children and takes particular delight in giving young people a head start and coaching them to success.

Take R.J. Watkins, for example. He was a high school dropout who wanted to be a radio and TV producer with his own business. But banks weren't exactly lining up to give him the money he needed to create his dream. Then he crossed paths with Keys.

"I'm successful today because of Brady Keys's help," said Watkins. "He's an angel to me."

Without Keys's financial backing, Watkins said, no bank was going to loan him money to start his business. That was more than a decade ago. Today, the Detroit, Michigan, production company that Keys helped him set up has several programs in syndication—on radio, TV, and video.

"I'm going to do everything in my power to keep this going as long as I live," Watkins said of his business. "I'd do anything not to let him down."

Watkins is part of a large and devoted following who can trace the turning points in their lives to Keys. Another is Brenda Ramsey, a former restaurant employee, who launched a chain of hair-styling salons with Keys's help. Starting in Detroit, she ambitiously expanded her business to other parts of the country, including Albany, with Keys's encouragement.

Ramsey said she thinks of Keys like a father. "He pushes you to see your own potential and then lets you do what you can do. He likes most to help people develop their own skills. But if you run into problems, you can always run back to him. You can call him anytime you need anything."

Though some may doubt Keys's motivations for gambling on unproven business risks, he is driven by a simple and sincere desire "to take care of the people who have helped me get where I am," he said. "I feel that's what God wants me to do.

"I'm not out to make a lot of business conquests," he added. "I turn down deals all the time."

Those who know him say that's not bragging, it's just the facts.

"You wouldn't think an ex–football player would be as unassuming as he is," said John Richards, a reporter for the Albany newspaper who's written about Keys. Even though Keys has been active in the community, setting up a TV program designed to keep kids away from drugs and sponsoring entertainment events for young people, he "doesn't toot his own horn," Richards added.

That's how Keys wants it. People "will see who I am through my deeds," he explained, "not by what I say."

Marie G. Lee

★ *My parents have always instilled in me the belief that anything is possible, and if I can pass this gift on through my writing or through my personal relationships, I'll consider myself a success.*

Marie G. Lee had taken the biggest gamble of her life and it looked like she might lose everything.

Since grade school, she'd wanted to be a writer. But as Lee matured, she shelved her childhood ambition in favor of a more secure profession—economics. At 25, Lee was, by most accounts, a success: she had a degree from a leading college and a budding career on Wall Street.

But she wasn't satisfied. Lee's desire to put words on paper was not a youthful fantasy to be outgrown. So in every spare moment she continued to practice her craft, pushing herself in an around-the-clock pace that at one point put her in the hospital.

In time, Lee came to terms with a tough realization: she had to take a chance on her dream. She decided to forfeit her full-time job to finish the novel she'd started—the story of Ellen Sung, a Korean-American teen who wants to be popular but struggles with racism and pressures of all kinds from both peers and her parents, while she completes her senior year of high school.

Banking her life and livelihood on that book was one of the most risky, and rewarding, choices Lee ever made.

"During the years I tried to sell my first novel, I received a lot of nice letters from editors who thought I wrote well, but who also thought the book itself would never sell," Lee said. "In that time, I wrote another book with an Asian-American character, and when *that* didn't sell well either, I panicked: I was well on my way to poverty. But I sat down and started on the third.

134

"No matter what it took, I wanted to write the books that *I* wanted to read, but could never find as a kid."

Growing up in a Minnesota mining town, Lee endured a special brand of isolation and loneliness. Her family bore the dubious distinction of being the only Korean-Americans in Hibbing; Lee sought escape from the confines of her working-class community by picking up books. But even in those imaginary worlds, she longed for a companionship she couldn't find: characters who, like her, were caught between two cultures, attempting to reconcile an all-American upbringing with an ethnic heritage that, at the very least, made them look different.

"As a kid, I was often nervous in social situations, so reading books was a private, wonderful time for me: just me and the characters in the book," Lee said.

The third of four children, two boys and two girls, Lee remembers her childhood as a largely happy time. But she also acknowledges that from a very early age, her life was directed by two strong undercurrents: racism and the pressures of being a second-generation Asian-American. Lee's family had settled in Hibbing because a friend of her immigrating parents got her father a job there as an anesthesiologist.

"We were the only Asian-American family in a town that otherwise was pretty much all-white. Nothing dramatic ever happened: no one burned crosses on our lawn or anything, but things did happen," Lee recalled.

"The worst was when a teacher—beloved by everyone in the school—started making subtle anti-Asian jokes in front of the class. I really feel rotten about this because I didn't stand up for myself at the time—I was too cowed by authority. But if I had, I could have brought attention to the fact that this very smart, charming man was at the same time alarmingly racist," Lee said.

"The second worst thing was being asked to leave a graduation party—on *my* graduation night—by a drunk redneck who said the party was only for 'Americans.' "

Such episodes were balanced by the love and support of friends and family who nurtured Lee's self-esteem.

"My parents were especially keen on imparting to us kids the value of learning. No expenses were spared. They brought us tire-

135

lessly to the library, and even paid us—pennies, that is—to read books. For me, this was heaven," Lee said.

"The other invaluable thing my parents did was to allow me 'free thinking time.' I have friends whose parents think that a still kid is an idle kid, and even the sight of a kid reading a book can drive them to send the kid out to mow the lawn, to camp, whatever," Lee said. "My parents, however, were content to let me lie around and stare into space a lot, especially during summers, and I doubt I would have become a writer had I not had this time."

Even as an amateur author, Lee demonstrated the industriousness that has fueled her success. "I knew I wanted to be a writer ever since I got my first typewriter—a clunky, manual hand-me-down—and saw how cool the words looked when they were typed," she said. "My first book was made out of scratch paper and was held together by yarn."

She was 8, and it would take another eight years before the ambitious Lee actually was published: at 16, she sold an essay to *Seventeen* magazine. By then, she recalled, "my drawers were crammed full of finished stories, and being published in a real magazine was the best encouragement."

At the same time, by nature and by upbringing, Lee was practical. "My parents did not push me to become a writer," Lee said. "Actually, like a lot of Asian-American parents—especially since my father was a doctor—they were sort of hoping one of us kids would follow in his footsteps."

Lee did comply with one expectation: that she would graduate from college equipped to earn a living. "Writing was the most natural thing for me to do—it was like breathing," Lee said. "However, like breathing, it did not promise financial security."

So Lee steered her life in another direction. Attending Brown University in Providence, Rhode Island, she studied for a career in economics. But even after graduating with top honors, Lee never forgot her dream—she just didn't feel ready to pursue writing as a profession.

"Some of it, I have to admit, is that I didn't want my parents to worry," she said. "It's not that I didn't have faith in myself—but I really don't think you can just sit down and say 'I want to be a writer.' I felt I needed to get out and work and experi-

Marie Lee

ence life, because I believe you have to pay some dues."

For Lee, that meant almost five years in New York's financial district. Her first job was at a firm that did econometric forecasting; in college, Lee had specialized in this highly technical field, which uses mathematical and statistical methods to develop economic theories.

"This was something I really had studied hard for," she said of her first position, which involved working on a computer and preparing reports. "But I wasn't terribly good at it," Lee said. "I think I forced myself to do it and I had a certain level of competence with it."

Pushing herself to "write like a demon," plus handle a professional position drove Lee to exhaustion and a hospital bed in 1987. Suffering from a full-blown case of mononucleosis, she went home to Minnesota for a month to rest and recuperate.

But she returned to New York, determined to pick up where she'd left off. After two and a half years in econometrics, Lee made a career move, accepting a job at Goldman Sachs, an investment bank where her responsibilities focused on research and editing financial reports. Though her work continued to be more technical than creative, Lee didn't mind, for she had begun to dedicate all her free time to writing. "I would write for a couple of hours before I went to work, and then I would write when I got home," she said. "And I'd write on the weekends."

Goldman Sachs not only provided the requisite paycheck; it proved a perfect contrast to her alter ambition. "In some ways, a job like that is good because it doesn't take the writing away from you during the day," Lee said. "If I had been working in publishing, it would have been harder for me—but this stuff was just dry and statistical."

She began working in earnest on her first young adult novel, the story of high school senior Ellen Sung. But perhaps more importantly, Lee forced herself to put every extra cent from her paycheck into savings. She was planning her escape from the world of high finance—but the ever-sensible Lee knew she'd never survive without a sizable nest egg to live on until she sold her first book.

Almost two years after joining Goldman Sachs, Lee made her leap of faith, quitting her job to devote all her time to writing. In 1989, after much writing, rewriting and polishing, her manuscript was ready. But finding a publisher proved to be an agonizingly slow process punctuated by rejection letters that Lee filed away one by one. All told, her novel was turned down by fifteen publishers and agents, many of whom thought no one would want to read about an Asian-American girl coming of age. "Plus they thought my treatment of racism was rather bald," Lee said.

All the while, she continued to write, completing a second book.

Set in seventh grade, it's the story of "a Korean adoptee who's pretty much brought up thinking she's white until a Korean kid comes to her school, and she has an identity crisis," Lee explained.

While Lee was peddling her first book and plugging away on her second, America's demographics were changing. The literary world began to take note of writers who could address racial diversity with sensitivity and candor. In a happy coincidence, the demands of the marketplace collided with Lee's lifelong dream: in 1992, in a matter of months, she saw her first book published, sold her second, and received an advance from her publisher to write a third.

"Multicultural literature was barely a gleam in an editor's eye," Lee said, when she started her first novel in 1986. "Now, everybody is saying 'Oh, we've needed a book like this for so long.' This trend has helped me immensely—even though it's the same manuscript I've had for years."

Publicly, Lee may appear to have just burst onto the young adult literary scene, a prolific new voice cranking out one book after another. But behind the scenes, Lee's private fan club of family and friends are exhaling a collective sigh of relief that her risk paid off.

"If you only knew what she's gone through," said long-time friend Mary Kim. "She's a very private person who doesn't complain, but she's the hardest worker I know.

"A lot of people profess to have the dream of being a writer," said Kim, who is a volunteer with a Korean-American writers' organization that's promoting Lee's first book. "I sometimes think when people meet Marie they believe that because she doesn't have a job, she's having a good time. But for her, writing is gut-wrenching work that she pours her heart and soul into."

Even Lee candidly acknowledges that sheer will power and faith kept her going during the decade between teenage essayist and self-supporting novelist. In between were many opportunities for self-doubt.

"After ten years of writing with nothing remarkable to show for it, I had to face the fact that I had no job to speak of, and nothing to show for all the higher education my parents had paid for, and there was the possibility that I might never publish the two novels I'd written," Lee said.

"Many well-meaning people—after watching me sweat over this

for years, succumb to mono, become depressed—gently suggested that I should look further, do corporate writing, go back to graduate school.

"Now that both my novels have been sold and I'm rounding out the third, things are looking pretty good. But just a year ago, during my second year of unemployment, I really started to feel I was looking into a dark tunnel."

Lee, now 28, is disarmingly matter-of-fact when discussing her success. Clearly she's delighted with how her writing career has taken off. But equally apparent is the fact that she made it happen, moment by moment, through discipline and a determination to hold onto her dream for dear life.

"I think one of the problems that I see in today's kids is an unwillingness to accept delayed gratification," Lee said. "Because if you truly want something you have to sacrifice and really work hard on it, *and get rejected*—and I feel like people just aren't willing to do that. They just go through life with an avoidance of pain."

Though writing is her life's passion, Lee faces each day with a measure of fear that maybe she won't be able to get the words down—or worse yet, that her words won't capture the emotion or experience she wants to share with readers. "A lot of times the most enjoyment I get out of life is when I'm writing and it's going well," she said. "But I also find it very daunting to face a blank page all the time."

Just as when she was a kid, Lee regularly produces reams of copy. In addition to novels, she's written numerous articles that have appeared in *YM,* the *Brown Alumni Monthly,* and *The New York Times.* In fact, Lee's so prolific that when she traces the evolution of various projects, sometimes it's hard to tell where one leaves off and another begins.

For instance, she wrote three eighty-page drafts of her second book, thinking it should be a sequel to her first. "Then I realized finally that this was a waste of time, and I threw it away," she said. Similarly, between her second and third books, she wrote a four-hundred-page adult book "that's so horrible I'm just chalking it up to experience," she said. That went into the trash too.

"I make a lot of mistakes along the way," Lee said, adding that it's hard to strike the balance between not giving up too easily and being able to recognize when something really isn't working. "A lot of times I'll force myself to finish something because if I say 'This is no good' and throw it away, I'd never get anything done."

When she's writing a book, Lee goes into a creative isolation that directs all her energies, emotional and physical, into the project. She regularly puts in twelve-hour days that begin at dawn and unfold with a practiced rhythm. From 5:30 to 7, she writes, then takes a quick breakfast break, and continues writing till midday. After lunch, she goes running and may take a nap, before resuming work in late afternoon. "If I'm really manic about it, I'll work late into the night and drink a lot of coffee," Lee said.

This ability to completely absorb herself in her work with unwavering discipline has been a driving force in Lee's success. "Writing is probably the hardest profession to get into except, perhaps, for being an astronaut," Lee said.

"On the other hand, you can't let odds deter you. If someone would have come up with a scientific study that predicted that I, Marie Lee, had a one-in-one-hundred-thousand chance of becoming a published writer—and that it would take ten years—I would have tried to ignore it and just kept plugging away."

Lee credits her parents as "the single biggest influence in my success." She also benefited from some expert advice and mentoring at critical points in her career. Possibly one of the most inspired moves Lee made early on was to write a letter to her favorite childhood author, Judy Blume. Lee enclosed samples of her work and shared her dream of writing books for young adults, like Blume.

The elder author responded, offering to put Lee in touch with her agent and editor. "The only advice I can offer is keep writing," Blume wrote. "Don't give up easily. It takes time and perseverance, and writing is hard, lonely work."

Today the two authors are friends. "Judy Blume basically gave me pure, unadulterated encouragement—which really helped a lot, especially when I was being rejected," Lee said. "She just kept saying that I was a great writer and I should keep going. And that really did help me keep going."

Another pivotal moment occurred at a 1989 writing workshop when teacher Nancy Willard "took an interest in my book," Lee said. "She went far beyond the call of duty."

141

Though Lee's first novel was already being shopped around to publishers, Willard suggested reworking some sections. During the conference, Lee followed Willard's counsel with rewarding results: "She thought the revision was so great," Lee recalled, "she read it in front of the class and everybody clapped. That was definitely a time in my writing where I made a turning point. It really just changed my writing forever."

Like many beginning authors, Lee draws heavily on her own experience, and can even pinpoint the moment when the idea for her first novel, *Finding My Voice,* came to her.

"I was back home in Minnesota, and my dad and I were driving to go skiing," she recalled. "We were going through the town of Biwabik—the name even sounds small—and I saw two guys in football letter jackets walking down the main street. I thought to myself, I want to write a story that will capture all this: what it's like to live in the snow and the cold, what it's like being in these small towns where everybody knows everybody, and having a letter jacket means you are really *something.*

"That was the idea," Lee said. "As I wrote the book, the themes of fitting in, racism, peer and parental pressure all sort of inserted themselves. As I remember it, high school was the time I felt my emotions extra intensely, and for all its ups and downs, I still think of my high school years as some of the best in my life."

Much of what happens to Ellen Sung, the main character, during her senior year at Arkin High in Minnesota mirrors Lee's experiences. "Like most other kids, she wants to fit in, have fun, and maybe even find a boyfriend. She has a lot of friends, but there are some people who don't like her just because she's Asian," Lee said.

"Arkin is a small mining town, and everyone is white, except for her family. Perhaps because of this, her parents push her extra hard to become 'American,' and as a result, Ellen not only feels that she can't tell her parents about how some of the other kids—and teachers—are treating her, but she also feels shut out of her own history."

Early reviews of *Finding My Voice* praised Lee's treatment of these complex concerns.

"This portrait of a quietly sensitive teenager is filled with searing truths about day-to-day racism—those that don't make the evening news," said a writer in one of the prestigious "pointer" columns in *Kirkus Review.* "Honestly rendered, and never didactic, the story allows readers first to flinch in recognition, and then to look into their own hearts."

Publishers Weekly said, "The author's depiction of first-generation anxieties demonstrates depth and candor, two hallmarks of this sensitive book."

Like her main character, Lee survived the pain of prejudice through the encouragement of "strong, close friends who helped me see that these names had little to do with me as a person," she said. "Looking back, I see that there was real potential for me as an impressionable adolescent to lose my self-esteem because of some things that people said.

"And if I hadn't had the support of my parents and friends, perhaps I would've just become a bitter, hateful person instead of having the experience make me learn to stand up for myself."

That's why Lee has chosen to write for young adults—"because people's prejudices get fixed as they get older, so it's good to reach kids," she said.

"I hope the book will make anyone who has been the target of any kind of prejudice realize that it is something outside themselves that inspires this kind of hate, and that they have the right to exist along with everybody else," Lee said.

"I also hope the book will make people think twice before they say something they really don't mean."

Spike Lee

★ | *I'm doing this because I want to make films and I love filmmaking—I would hope that when my epitaph is written, it will just say that I was a brother who wanted to make good films.*

One night during his junior year at Morehouse College in Atlanta, crammed into a taxi with college buddies on their way back to campus after seeing *The Deer Hunter,* Spike Lee turned to a friend and declared: "I know what I want to do. I want to make films." From that night on, his friend would later remark, "Spike was a monomaniac with a mission."

That single-minded mania has forged a new genre of moviemaking. Not only has Shelton Jackson "Spike" Lee made some very good movies (almost one controversial blockbuster a year since 1985), but he is credited with shattering Hollywood barriers for black filmmakers.

Lee's gritty cinematic style has redefined moviemaking in tinsel town and opened doors for a new generation of black directors intent on producing hard-edged, uncompromising films about black life in America. In an industry where demand for profits often dictates the art, it was Lee who finally forced Hollywood executives to acknowledge what they had long refused to believe: films made by blacks about blacks can pack theaters with diverse audiences—and score huge box office receipts.

In doing so, Lee established himself as an outspoken champion of black filmmakers. Black directors, he insists, are the people best able to portray the diverse, complex experiences of being black in America, and he's harshly critical of attempts by Hollywood's anointed white directors to do so.

Lee, who writes, acts, produces, and directs, said his mission is "to put the vast richness of black culture on film. Movies are the most powerful medium in the world and we just can't sit back and let other people define our existence, especially when they're putting lies out there on the screen."

Such a contentious point of view leaves few people unopinionated about Lee's directorial talents. Fans praise him as one of the most innovative, provocative filmmakers to come along in years; his detractors berate him for what they see as angry, racist grandstanding. Meanwhile, moviegoers flock to his films, clearly hungry for movies with characters and plots that don't condescend or stereotype.

"I get attention because I'm black and making films about black people," Lee said. "But it's not different than a Jewish director making films about Jewish people or those who are products of their background, upbringing, and experiences who decide to make a film about something they believe in."

Through his films, Lee explores a wide and complex range of issues, from promiscuity and love in *She's Gotta Have It* (1985) and black-on-black prejudices in *School Daze* (1988), to racial tensions in *Do the Right Thing* (1989) and interracial relationships in *Jungle Fever* (1991)

Those are touchy subjects across America—and they're ones that Lee confronts with such dramatic realism that moviegoers squirm uncomfortably in their seats while critics debate whether he should be hailed for his artistic vision or lambasted for racist and sexist imagery.

In pursuit of his vision, Lee has shown little restraint in his willingness to offend almost anyone—white or black. He was almost thrown out of film school when he produced a pointed critique of the racism in D.W. Griffith's silent film classic *The Birth of a Nation*. White critics have openly worried that his films would incite race riots. Blacks have chastised him for shallow portrayals of black women and "backward sexual politics."

But Lee doesn't back down. "Spike likes to fight," said writer Nelson George, a friend of Lee's and an original investor in *She's Gotta Have It*. "There's a gleeful look he gets, a certain kind of excitement in his eyes, when shit is being stirred up."

Lee's mother, Jacquelyn, must have seen that look early on: she

Spike Lee

coined the nickname "Spike" for her firstborn because he was such a tough little baby.

Family has been a powerful influence in Lee's life and work. Sister Joie and brother Cinque act in his movies, and another brother, David, is the unit photographer. His father, acclaimed jazz bassist and composer Bill Lee, has scored the music for every film.

The elder Lee made sure all five of his children knew their family history, taking them on annual car trips from New York to Alabama and Georgia to visit grandparents. Bill Lee's grandfather had overcome poverty and a crippling bone disease to study at the famous

Tuskegee Institute in Alabama; he eventually founded his own institute to educate black youth.

That emphasis on education continued with each generation. Both of Spike Lee's parents attended college: his father earned a degree from Morehouse; his mother was educated at nearby Spelman.

"Spike was always real tight with his family," said his best friend, Monty Ross. "The men really stick together, take care of business. To know your lines, those generations — to have history — that's a very powerful thing."

When Lee was a sophomore at Morehouse College, his mother died suddenly of liver cancer. Ever since, his grandmother, Zimmie, who lives in Atlanta and is known by her grandchildren simply as Mama, has been there to help him through the tough times — emotionally and financially.

At Morehouse, Lee devoted himself to extracurricular activities — writing for the school newspaper, working as a disc jockey at a local jazz radio station, and directing the school's lavish coronation pageant on homecoming weekend during his senior year. He also bought his first super-8 camera and began experimenting with filmmaking.

Lee's first serious artistic recognition as a filmmaker came during his final year as a graduate student at New York University's prestigious film school. His master's thesis project was an hourlong color film titled *Joe's Bed-Stuy Barbershop: We Cut Heads.* A wryly humorous and realistic look at ghetto life, the film received a student Academy Award from the Academy of Motion Picture Arts and Sciences. The film also became the first student production selected for Lincoln Center's "New Directors/New Films" series, and it was aired on public television's "Independent Focus" series.

Despite the movie's success and critical acclaim, no Hollywood job offers came after Lee received his master's degree in filmmaking from NYU in 1982. The experience, Lee remembered, "cemented in my mind what I always thought all along: that I would have to go out and do it alone, not rely on anyone else."

Going it alone, Lee soon learned that commercial success didn't come easily. His first attempt at independent filmmaking was a drama called *Messenger.* Eight weeks into production, during the summer of 1984, Lee had to kill his movie about a New York City bicycle messenger because he got into a dispute with the Screen Actors Guild.

Lee lost $40,000 on the project, but didn't lose his drive to make films. A year later he was filming the comedy *She's Gotta Have It.* Lee shot the film in twelve days, mostly in a small Brooklyn apartment and nearby park, on a paltry budget of $175,000—chump change by Hollywood moviemaking standards. Lee scraped the money together while he was still producing the film by asking everyone he knew if they would like to invest.

"We never knew where the next nickel was going to come from, so we wrote to or called everybody we knew in the world, asking them to send money, even if it was just $50," he said. "Each day while we were shooting, someone would go back to my house to see if any checks had come and then rush them to the bank, and we'd just hope they'd clear in time."

The scramble paid off. *She's Gotta Have It* launched Lee into moviemaking stardom and made a lot of money.

Audiences loved Lee's low-budget debut about the life of a young black woman and her relationships with three very different lovers. When *She's Gotta Have It* premiered at a film festival in San Francisco, viewers gave it a standing ovation. Film distribution companies rushed to pick up *She's Gotta Have It,* and it became the first movie by an independent black filmmaker in almost fifteen years to receive major international distribution. The movie grossed $1.8 million in three weeks, eventually bringing in more than $7 million.

The success of *She's Gotta Have It* caught the interest of major studios. Columbia Pictures gave Lee $6 million to produce his next film, *School Daze,* which dealt with his experiences as a student at Morehouse College and the seldom-discussed prejudices that exist between light-skinned and dark-skinned blacks. Lee planned to film the movie at Morehouse, but school officials, disturbed by Lee's depiction of blacks and black colleges, asked him to leave after three weeks of shooting. Undaunted, Lee completed the film at a nearby college. But the film's controversial subject matter prompted the United Negro College Fund to cancel plans for a benefit premiere.

Despite the controversy, Lee never faltered from his mission: "This film is about our existence, about being black in white America, and to me, there is nothing more important than that."

School Daze became a commercial success, and a scene from the movie even spawned a new dance craze called "da butt." The song that accompanied the dance scene also became a hit record.

Lee continued to create controversy with his subsequent films. Critics of *Do the Right Thing* assailed Lee for promoting violence as a means of fighting injustice. Some even feared that the film would spark race riots. Lee countered that *Do the Right Thing* wasn't made to incite riots, "but to provoke discussion about racism, which is something people do not want to talk about."

After making three controversial hits in four years, Lee took a break in 1990 by producing the jazz film *Mo' Better Blues*. But a year later he was stirring things up again. Delving into black-white race taboos, he produced *Jungle Fever*, an interracial scorcher about a love affair between a black architect and his white secretary.

Lee's latest project, *Malcolm X*, is his biggest-budget movie to date—about $33 million—and his most controversial.

Since 1968, repeated attempts to tell the complex life story of this assassinated black nationalist leader have invariably become mired in controversy. During the making of *Malcolm X*, Lee became the focus of much attention as both admirers and critics debated whether he would be able to capture Malcolm on film. Lee rewrote a screenplay by James Baldwin and Arnold Perl, and the movie opened in November 1992.

In his inimitable style, Lee fields the flak over whether he is capable of handling the project: "Somebody could definitely be killed behind this movie," he quipped. "Hopefully, it won't be me."

Whatever viewers ultimately think of the film, Lee, as usual, is prepared to take full responsibility. "Everybody has their own Malcolm who is dear to them," Lee said. "All I can say is this: I was the director, I rewrote the script by James Baldwin and Arnold Perl, and I will take full responsibility. I will say that this is the Malcolm I see."

Meanwhile, Lee continues to broaden his influence, seemingly working around the clock. Among his other credits are commercials, music videos, books, albums, and a line of Spike Lee clothing, and video and film memorabilia. He runs his own film production company, Forty Acres and a Mule Filmworks, and a retail store in the Brooklyn neighborhood where he was raised. Lee also has tried his hand at teaching film at Harvard University and Long Island University, and he's funded scholarships at his alma maters, Morehouse College and New York University.

It's an impressive list of accomplishments for someone only in his 30s. But Lee stays clearly focused on his mission because there's so much more yet to do.

"Black filmmaking is still lagging," Lee said. "When you compare what we've done in film to the other art forms, it's really minuscule. We're in the embryonic stages of film when you compare it to what we've done in sports, dance, music, art. Black cinema has produced no Charlie Parkers yet, no John Coltranes, no James Baldwins, no Paul Robesons. We will, but we're not at that level yet."

The way Lee sees it, he's simply trying to carry on the work started by such black predecessors as Oscar Micheaux, Ossie Davis, Gordon Parks, and Melvin Van Peebles. Without them, he said, "there would be no Spike Lee, the filmmaker. They handed me the baton. I'm trying to run with it a little while before I have to give it up."

Wilma Mankiller

 I want to be remembered as the person who helped us restore faith in ourselves.

Starting with her surname, Wilma Mankiller's life is one of contrasts. At 47, she is a soft-spoken, serene grandmother. At the same time, as the first female chief of the Cherokee Nation, which numbers some 140,000 members, she is a fierce fighter for her people's rights.

Although she is a feminist, Mankiller's name should not be taken literally. It is derived from a high Cherokee military rank that a male ancestor adopted many years ago as the family name.

Using her position as a forum for Indians to solve their social problems, Mankiller at first faced resistance from male members of her tribe. "I've run into more discrimination as a woman than as an Indian," said Mankiller, who compares her job to running a small country or a medium-sized corporation.

She is an unlikely politician, who admits that playing the game in Washington is the most unappealing part of her job. She prefers staying home, where she can tackle situations in a straightforward, hands-on manner.

Half Cherokee and half Caucasian, Mankiller has the dark hair and complexion of her Indian father, but the stature and facial features of her Dutch-Irish mother. She spent her early childhood on a 160-acre tract of land called Mankiller Flats in Adair County, Oklahoma.

The Cherokees were removed to Indian Territory, now Oklahoma, by the United States government in 1838–39. The forced removal by President Andrew Jackson's military troops ended with more than four thousand of the sixteen thousand Cherokees dead.

When the federal government decided to open Indian Territory to white settlers, the land of the Cherokees was taken away and tribal members were given allotments. The land where Mankiller's home now stands was allotted to her grandfather by the United States government in 1907, when Oklahoma became the forty-sixth state in the union.

Mankiller grew up among six siblings, and like most Indians, her family lived in abject poverty. Conveniences such as indoor plumbing and electricity were almost unknown.

When Mankiller was 11, her family's farm was nearly destroyed after suffering two years of severe drought. Her father, seeking help to rebuild the farm, was turned away by the government; instead, he was encouraged to enter the Bureau of Indian Affairs' relocation program.

"Relocation was yet another answer from the federal government to the continuing dilemma of what to do with us," said Mankiller. "We are a people with many, many social indicators of decline and an awful lot of problems, so in the fifties, they decided to mainstream us—to try to take us away from the tribal land and the tribal culture, get us into the cities. It was supposed to be a better life."

The Mankillers accepted the government's offer and moved to San Francisco, where they experienced severe culture shock. "One day I was here and the next I was trying to deal with the mysteries of television, indoor plumbing, neon lights, and elevators," said Mankiller, who now lives in Oklahoma.

True to his proud heritage, Mankiller's father persevered and rose to the top, at first becoming a warehouse worker, then a union activist. Mankiller said her father was "the only full-blooded Indian union activist."

During the sixties, Mankiller studied sociology and became a social worker. She married a wealthy Ecuadorian accountant and gave birth to two daughters. Her interest in Indian rights was ignited in 1969, when a group of young Indian demonstrators took over the abandoned Alcatraz prison in San Francisco Bay to call attention to the deplorable treatment of American Indians.

"Those college students who participated in Alcatraz articulated a lot of feelings I had that I'd never been able to express," she said.

During the protesters' eighteen-month occupation, Mankiller helped raise funds to support their cause. Because of her responsibilities as a mother, she didn't participate in the protest directly— but the Alcatraz experience changed her.

Wilma Mankiller

From that time on, Indian identity became a guiding theme in her life: she went back to college at night and became the native American programs coordinator for the Oakland, California, public school system. Then in the mid-seventies, she divorced her husband and returned to Oklahoma to claim her grandfather's land.

"I wanted my children to experience the rural life," she said. "And I thought some of the skills I'd learned out there [in San Francisco], I could practice here." She built a small wooden house on Mankiller Flats, where she still lives.

In 1977, she became economic stimulus coordinator for the Cherokee Nation. Using her social work skills, Mankiller introduced a self-help project to the Cherokees. She reminded her people that taking responsibility for change builds self-esteem.

"My goal has always been for Indians to solve their own economic problems," she said. In 1979, she became program development specialist for the Cherokee Nation; and in 1981, she founded the Community Development Department of the Cherokee Nation, becoming its director after raising funds for its establishment.

As director, she stressed self-help and began several innovative programs, including the development of rural water systems and the rehabilitation of housing. She perceived herself merely as a resource who showed her people how to define problems. Thanks to her guidance and example, today, if they want a community building, they plan the project and erect it themselves.

Mankiller believes there is something almost patronizing about an organization—even when it's your own tribal government—deciding what people need, going to Washington for funds, and then applying those funds to a community, without working with local leaders.

"I'd like to see whole, healthy communities again," she said, emphasizing the empowerment of the people on a local level. "One of the biggest problems is that we need to really trust our own selves and our own thinking, and not to allow others to convince us that our thoughts, ideas, and plans and visions aren't valid."

Mankiller has put self-help principles to work in her personal life as well, after being seriously injured in a head-on collision in 1979. Following the accident, she underwent seventeen operations to correct physical problems caused by the crash.

During the treatment, she discovered she had myasthenia gravis, a muscular disease. It was like getting a one-two punch, but Mankiller came back with a few swings of her own. Enduring an operation and lengthy treatments, she succeeded in sending the disease into remission.

"Everything has been up from that point on," she said, recalling the ordeal. "In a way, it seems it was a test of perseverance or something that I went through. It was a maturing kind of process. It was a definite preparation." (In 1990, Chief Mankiller survived another major operation—a kidney transplant. Her brother, Don, was the donor. Since returning to Oklahoma, she has drawn on her talent for writing proposals. She applied for and obtained a number of grants for social service projects such as Cherokee Gardens, a successful gardening business.)

Mankiller's initiative attracted the attention of her tribe's chief, Ross Swimmer. In 1983, he selected her as his running mate in the tribal elections—despite what might seem to be obvious philosophical differences. He was a conservative Republican banker; she described herself as a liberal Democrat.

But their ticket triumphed, making Mankiller the first woman elected to the post of deputy chief. As a team, they concentrated on getting the Cherokee tribe to be less dependent on government handouts, and on reducing friction between full-blooded and mixed-blood members.

When Swimmer was appointed in 1985 by President Reagan to head the Bureau of Indian Affairs in Washington, D.C., Mankiller became the first woman chief of the Cherokees—a monumental event in their history. Two years later, she ran for election and won in her own right.

Although the Cherokees, like many North American Indian tribes, were originally female-oriented in lifestyle and descent, their contact with white men eventually led to an exclusively male system of government. Traditionally, women chose the chiefs, who served at their pleasure. And rather than having great debates in the council meetings, women were consulted beforehand on what the issues would be.

"Early historians referred to our government as a petticoat government because of the strong role of women in the tribe," said Mankiller. "Then we adopted a lot of ugly things that were part of the non-Indian world, and one of those things was sexism."

Specifically, it was after the Trail of Tears that women became subservient. Under the enormous stress of relocation, the Cherokees internalized the cultural values of the dominant society. It was ironic that in 1687, Cherokee women enjoyed a prominent role in government, but by 1987, tribespeople questioned whether women should hold leadership positions.

"So my election was a step forward and a step backward at the same time," said Mankiller, whose second husband, Charlie Soap, is a Cherokee fluent in the native language and involved in rural development. He helped convince fellow tribesmen that it was "safe" to have his wife running the Cherokee Nation.

Conscious of being the first female chief, Mankiller has worked extra hard to succeed. She's focused on basics, such as reducing a fifty-percent unemployment rate among the Cherokee population, raising educational levels, and improving health care, as well as the economic development of northeastern Oklahoma. An aggressive business-development team works in tandem with area chambers of commerce to attract new business to the region.

"The businesses we want to attract have got to have good environmental records," Mankiller said. "It's not worth the long-term damage to the environment for the short-term benefit of providing jobs."

But there are still many forces working against the Indians. Mankiller has used her position to tell the story of the Cherokee Nation, bring nationwide attention to Indian issues, and help erase common stereotypes.

"Many think we're either visionaries, 'noble savages,' squaw drudges, or tragic alcoholics," said Mankiller. Even in nearby Tulsa, there are people oblivious to the fact that Cherokees exist in neighboring communities, and that they have a thriving language and viable tribal government. Mankiller is frustrated that Cherokees are rarely depicted as real people struggling to hang on to their culture and values in a society that neutralizes ethnic differences.

"On the contrary, we are a revitalized tribe, we have kept the best of our old way of life and incorporated the sounder elements of today's non-Indian world," said Mankiller, who epitomizes that philosophy.

Although her bookshelves are filled with works by Plato, Chaucer, and Tolstoy, she is as likely to go to a medicine man as a doctor when she gets a cold. Although she is a powerful advocate for Indian rights in Washington, she most enjoys the rural life with her children and grandchildren.

With her roots nourished in Oklahoma soil, Mankiller keeps promoting self-help as the key to Cherokee survival in the twenty-first century and beyond.

George L. Miles, Jr.

 All you need to do is find something you love to do and work as hard as you can at it. And you'll make your life a successful one.

One October day in 1987, George L. Miles, Jr., found himself in an unlikely spot for a top television executive. Sitting in a lifeboat with teenagers he'd just met an hour earlier, Miles was floating in circles in New York's East River.

Miles was part of a group leading the teens on a survival weekend in New York's "urban wilderness" as part of the city's Outward Bound program. He'd volunteered for the expedition because he liked the goals of Outward Bound—bringing together diverse people and helping them forge a unit through teamwork, cooperation, and resourcefulness. But crammed in that lifeboat—drifting left, drifting right, drawing circles in the river's chilly, murky waters— Miles wondered how he was going to get his crew of ten junior adventurers to navigate that boat up the river.

"A few of us realized we might spend a month in this boat," he recalled. "So we tried to rally the rest toward a common goal: something as easy as rowing a boat together. We did it, and for something this simple, all of us felt a sense of budding accomplishment."

Meeting goals is something Miles has a lot of experience in. After more than two decades of determined dreaming and hard work, Miles was offered the job of a lifetime. Today, at 52, he's the executive vice president and chief operating officer of WNET-TV in New York, the country's largest public television station.

"Years ago, I decided that what I wanted to do most was to contribute my fair share to my community," he said. "I got into public television because it serves the community in so many important ways, and I became a member of organizations that are committed to education and community service."

The man who leads the country's premier public television station has come a long way since his youth. He grew up during the 1940s and 1950s in Orange, New Jersey, in a housing project on Mechanic Street. By his own account, Miles was an average kid who became a successful adult because he made up his mind early on about the direction he wanted his life to go in.

But like that lifeboat in the East River, his life hasn't taken a straight path from Mechanic Street to the studios of WNET. He just always kept rowing, though, determined to reach his goals and lead a life he would find personally and professionally satisfying.

Miles's determination to succeed can be traced to his parents. Hardworking but uneducated—neither finished high school—they were determined that their seven children would have college educations. Miles's father, who worked as a shipping foreman, was a strict parent, always asking more of his children.

So after graduating from high school, Miles, who was the oldest of the kids, set off for Seton Hall University in South Orange, New Jersey. He majored in accounting, commuting back and forth between college and Mechanic Street, and working evenings and weekends for the YMCA, where he ran teen clubs and coached basketball.

College marked a turning point in his life, Miles said. He became the first in his family to earn a college degree—his four brothers followed in his footsteps. But he soon realized it was going to take more than a diploma to achieve his ambition of becoming a successful accountant with a major firm.

When he graduated college in 1963, big accounting firms simply weren't hiring blacks. Miles didn't let racism stop him, though.

"I had worked too long and too hard to give up," he said. "I was determined to build a good life and successful career, so I fought against that obstacle and found another route."

He took a job with the U.S. Department of Defense as a contract auditor. And, perhaps more importantly, he continued his education. While working for the government, he earned his master's degree in business at Fairleigh Dickinson University. He also served for two years in the military, including six months in Vietnam.

By 1969, there were more job opportunities for blacks. Still determined to realize his dream of being an accountant with a big firm,

George L. Miles, Jr.

Photo: Kate Kunz

Miles landed a job with Touche Ross & Co., one of the largest accounting firms in the country. "In the early sixties," he recalled, "they said 'you can't even get in here.'"

But his professional persistence paid off.

"It had taken me six years to do what I wanted to do, but I had persevered," Miles said, "and when the door opened, I was there."

Miles stayed with Touche Ross for eight years, wanting to prove his worth as a black man to fellow employees. His aim was to become a partner. But then he was invited to join Westinghouse

Broadcasting and Cable Inc. (Group W) as a station manager and controller for a TV and radio station in Pittsburgh, Pennsylvania. He accepted the offer.

"I took the job because it was an opportunity to combine the best of three worlds: business, community affairs, and competitiveness," he said.

Within two days of joining Group W, Miles said, he knew he had made the right decision because television offered everything he wanted. "A station's involved in its community," said Miles. "It can make a difference. It's competitive—and I'm as competitive as they come. And it pays a decent salary."

Miles's television career has been a steady succession of increasing responsibility in jobs that have taken him to numerous cities. After Pittsburgh he went to Charlotte, North Carolina, as a station manager and controller; then to New York as vice president and controller of the Westinghouse TV Group; and next, to Boston, as station manager at WBZ-TV, considered to be the strongest NBC affiliate in the country.

With each new assignment, his reputation as a skilled administrator grew. In 1983, the financially troubled National Public Radio in Washington, D.C., asked Miles for his help in sorting out and solving the station's money problems. Westinghouse agreed to give Miles a six-month leave of absence to serve as acting chief financial officer for National Public Radio.

Miles succeeded in helping NPR get back on a sound financial footing. And the following year, he was offered the biggest challenge of his career—leading New York's public television station, WNET, out of its own financial quagmire.

When Miles joined WNET as executive vice president and chief operating officer, the station had a budget deficit of $7 million. Since the nonprofit world of public television depends on donations from viewers and corporations for its survival, WNET clearly was in big trouble.

The station's board of trustees needed someone at the helm who knew the business of broadcasting, someone who could not only run a $100 million operation and eliminate the deficit, but also produce quality shows that would attract new viewers.

Miles was their man. Under his reign, WNET has introduced many popular programs that now reach 3.5 million viewers daily. He also has put the station's balance sheet in the black—WNET is not only financially sound, it has a financial surplus.

Miles said he was drawn to WNET, not just because of the station's prestige and influence, "but because the job requires two disciplines that many people mistakenly believe don't mix—understanding the goals of a nonprofit station, and at the same time, being astutely business-minded."

Miles describes himself as a high-energy person. For instance, he gets up at 5 A.M. to be at the office or gym by 7; often, he doesn't return home until 10 P.M. And he makes it a point to know most of the station's five hundred employees by name.

"I'm a guy without great talent," he said modestly. "So I make up for that by working hard and being disciplined and practicing."

Miles's favorite show on WNET is the *MacNeil/Lehrer News Hour,* which features news stories in depth. Five years ago, when he changed the program's starting time, it increased the viewing audience by 50 percent. Now some three hundred thousand people watch it regularly.

"That's a pretty good audience," said Miles, adding that he only wishes more people watched public television, in particular, his station.

"We're an active channel," he said. "You can't just cool out and vegetate by the hour."

Aware that people only watch WNET for an hour or two at a time—because the programs are so thought-provoking—Miles never stops promoting public television. "I do wish that we could activate more minds."

Despite his success, Miles hasn't forgotten Mechanic Street. At least four times a year, he makes it a point to return to his boyhood neighborhood, where people remember another Miles—not the highly respected television executive or certified public accountant.

"They knew me as a grubby little kid who at twelve years old used to play in the summertime with the other kids under the showers we'd put up between the buildings at the project," he said.

Back then, the projects were full of people from all backgrounds, Miles said. "We were a melting pot of blacks, Irish, and Italians 'just off the boat.' " He remembers how their building superintendent's wife taught his mother to make some of the best Italian food around.

Other things were different, too.

Miles, like most kids, got into trouble occasionally, but drugs weren't a major problem, he said. And though there were tussles between ethnic groups from time to time, the neighborhood was still like a family.

"I never forget where I came from," Miles said. When he's in Orange today, he either beeps his horn or stops to talk with people he knows. "No matter where I travel in the world, that's my home, and it always will be."

Because of his belief in the importance of family and community, Miles stays actively involved in organizations like Outward Bound. He is a firm believer in education and puts a lot of energy into serving as a role model for kids today.

A few years ago, Miles returned to his alma mater as the commencement speaker for Orange High School's graduating class of 1988. And for those few moments at the podium, he tried to teach them the lessons he's learned over a lifetime.

For one, there's no easy way to make dreams come true. "You've got to work at it day by day," Miles told the students.

And he shared three "simple but very powerful words:" choose, control, and connect.

"Choose the life that you want," he said. "And don't let anybody keep you from it.

"Control your mind, control your life, control your world. And look out for those who think they've got all the answers for you — because they probably don't. Nobody does," he cautioned.

"And finally, connect with the world. Work hard, and strive to be happy. You all deserve it."

Success, he told the seniors, comes from living the life you want to live, doing the things that make you happy.

"Success, like beauty, is in the eye of the beholder," he said. "It doesn't depend on the kind of work you do, or what title you have, or what salary you make. If you're getting everything out of life that you want, if you go to sleep at night feeling that you're doing the best you can, then you are successful.

"But you can't just sit back and wait for something to happen. Only *you* can make it happen."

Antonia Novello

> *I want to be able to look back someday and say, "I did make a difference." Whether it was to open the minds of people to think that a woman can do a good job, or whether it's the fact that so many kids out there think that they could be like me, then all the headaches and the chicken dinners will have been worth it.*

"Dreams sometimes come true in a strange way," Antonia Novello told President Bush when she was sworn into office as the Surgeon General of the United States in 1990. Her appointment to the highly visible post marked two important firsts: never before had a female or a Hispanic been given the responsibility as the doctor for all Americans.

"Dr. Novello's life is an amazing success story," President Bush declared. Accepting her new job before an enthusiastic crowd in the Roosevelt Room at the White House, Novello said, "The American dream is well and alive . . . today, *West Side Story* comes to the West Wing."

Novello's Washington, D.C., office is decorated with teddy bears and Cabbage Patch dolls, children's artwork and photos of youngsters, a collage of congratulatory notes from Puerto Rican schoolchildren, and quilts dedicated to two young people who died of AIDS — all mementos that showcase Novello's special interest and expertise in children.

Trained as a pediatrician and as a kidney specialist, the 47-year-old native of Puerto Rico holds one of the government's toughest jobs: making sure that everyone in the nation is healthy by promoting the best possible care, along with a strong dose of medical information.

163

"Good science and good sense" is Novello's motto and guiding force as she focuses on such critical issues as AIDS, alcohol and drug abuse, smoking, injury prevention, and domestic violence. And given her background, it's not surprising that she concentrates a good share of her efforts on women, children, teenagers, and minorities.

"Being a pediatrician, a woman, and a minority has helped me to do this job," she said.

In some ways, Novello has been training for this role her whole life. Born with an abnormally large colon, Novello, who was called "Tonito" as a small child, still remembers the pain of being a "sick kid."

"I was hospitalized every summer for at least two weeks," she recalled. "My pediatrician and my gastroenterologist [a specialist who treats stomach and intestinal disorders] were so nurturing and good to me that doctors became my buddies."

Although she was told she would need surgery to correct the problem when she reached her 8th birthday, "somebody in the medical field forgot," Novello said.

The university hospital was roughly thirty miles north of her tiny village, and during their many visits there, her mother, a school principal, pushed for an operation date. But it was not until Novello turned 18 that the operation became a reality. She had her surgery in the summer between her sophomore and junior years.

Even so, Novello isn't bitter or self-pitying. "Some people fall through the cracks," she said. "I was one of those."

In fact, perhaps because her mother never treated her like she was sick, Novello learned at a very young age to make the best of her situation. "Life issues you a hand," she said, "and you have to learn to play it."

As she spent her days in a hospital bed, Tonito toyed with a dream: she imagined herself as "a doctor for the little kids" in her hometown. But she kept her dream a secret. "It seemed too grand a notion," she recalled.

Ultimately, though, the inspiration and support of her mother and others turned her secret into a success story. "My pediatrician was kind," she recalled. "I wanted to be a doctor like him. My gastroenterologist was the dean of the medical school, and all my life, his was

Antonia Novello

the hand I saw — soothing and caring. And my favorite aunt was my nurse, and she was always saying, 'You have to be a doctor.' "

Even though Novello vowed she would never let anyone fall through the cracks like she did, and even though her biggest cheer-leader — her mother — encouraged her to go to college, she approached her doctor dream cautiously. She didn't tell anyone she had applied to medical school until after she was admitted. Looking back, she blames her hesitancy on "the typical attitude of women at that time—fear of failure."

Also, with her family being far from rich, she had no idea how she would pay for school. "But Mommy never panicked," Novello said. "When I told her I was accepted to medical school, she said that as long as there is a bank out there, we will find your tuition."

After graduating from the University of Puerto Rico Medical School in 1970, she married Joseph Novello. Now a Washington psychiatrist, he has described his wife as a woman "in whom Mother Teresa meets Margaret Thatcher."

She, in turn, credits his support in meeting her many goals. "It helps a lot to be married for twenty-two years," she said. "Not having children probably has helped because I don't feel so torn between kids who are at home and taking care of all the kids out there. More importantly, all of them have become my own."

Medical school was only the beginning of Novello's extensive education and training. While she was a first-year medical student her favorite aunt—the nurse—died of kidney failure. And Novello herself was hospitalized for a kidney ailment. The experience prompted her to seek more schooling to become a kidney specialist.

While a pediatric resident at the University of Michigan, Novello was cited for her outstanding performance in pediatrics and won the Intern of the Year Award.

In 1974, she opened her own pediatric practice. But she gave it up two years later. "When the pediatrician cries as much as the parents [of patients] do, then you know it's time to get out," she explained.

Her need to help more than one child turned into a crusade. Novello decided to go into public health service—a move that required yet more education. She earned a master of public health degree at the Johns Hopkins School for Public Health in Baltimore, Maryland. Those credentials launched Novello into a career that has given her ample opportunity to serve in public posts and earn a succession of professional honors.

In 1986, she was appointed deputy director of the National Institute of Child Health and Human Development. She also participated in a program for senior managers in government at the John F.

Kennedy School of Government at Harvard University.

At the time, Novello thought that she had reached the peak of her career. But just three years later, President Bush nominated her to be Surgeon General.

A petite figure in her navy blue uniform complete with shiny brass buttons and service medals, Novello has been described by some as "softspoken." Obviously, they do not know her—for Novello's message is strong and clear when she speaks out on her pet topics and targets.

Quick to go after cigarette makers, she called them part of "the self-serving, death-dealing tobacco industry and their soldiers of fortune, advertising agencies." Novello even dared to do something no other surgeon general had done: she held a news conference to take on R.J. Reynolds, the world's largest tobacco company, for trying to appeal to children with ads featuring Joe Camel, a cartoon character who is as recognizable as Mickey Mouse to preschoolers.

She also has attacked alcohol advertising, saying it "misleads, misinforms, and unabashedly targets youth," in order to rake in profits by promoting underage drinking. And she continually travels the country and appears on talk shows to educate people about the prevention of AIDS.

Novello insists, though, that the nation's health care isn't her concern alone. It takes everyone—parents, teachers, communities, police, and government—to protect, promote, and improve good health. Her special gift, she said, is "bureaucracy made easy," and her personal policy is to "remove fear, open doors, listen, educate, and assist."

She also is well known for her compassion for patients, a sensitivity acquired through her own chronic illness. Novello said her experiences as a kid made her "very conscious of how people feel when they are in bed as a patient."

She has become keenly aware of how medical professionals' overall attitude, behavior, and communication affect a patient's outlook on getting well. The doctors who score points with Novello are the ones who exemplify what being a doctor is all about—combining knowledge with compassion and sensitivity.

"I think the world of doctors who take time to play with a child, or bring him little presents and share time with him," Novello explained. "The best doctors are the ones who come into the room and talk to people like human beings."

Novello's struggles with serious illness as a child and later, as a medical student, not only taught her compassion but gave her the confidence it takes to do her job. Perhaps most importantly, she developed an enduring spirit out of the realization that a healthy sense of humor can make almost any situation bearable.

"If I can come back from surgery and go to college wearing Pampers for six months, I know nothing is going to pull me down. When I was in college with Pampers on, I used to laugh to myself, thinking, 'If they only knew.' At the same time, I gained more self-assurance and was able to say if I can survive that, I can do anything.

"I survived many times in my life," Novello said, "by learning to laugh at myself—that's the best medicine. But I also became very unsympathetic to those who misuse disease to gain sympathy."

Though her path to America's most prestigious medical post was paved with hardship and sometimes heartache, Novello forged ahead with a feisty spirit that has inspired many. And she offers this advice:

"Don't dwell on the negative. If you think a goal is unattainable—because you're African-American or Puerto Rican or female—it probably will be.

"Build on what you are, to become somebody."

Colin Powell

 Stay in school, get an education, and then take advantage of the opportunities this country offers.

When Colin Powell was in school during the 1950s, a military career wasn't a popular choice for most kids. But it was a way out of the Bronx, New York. And though he didn't realize it at the time, it was a smart choice for a black teenager because in those days, a person's race and religion often limited job possibilities.

Now, at 55, Powell is a four-star general who holds one of the most powerful positions in the country: Chairman of the Joint Chiefs of Staff. He is the youngest chairman in the history of the office, and the first black to hold the position.

Because of this, Powell is often asked to share his experiences as a minority member who has achieved considerable success by any standards.

As a youngster, Powell didn't think of himself as different. "Growing up in New York, particularly on Kelly Street in the South Bronx," said Powell, "everybody was a minority. You were either black, Puerto Rican, Jewish, or some European extraction."

His Bronx neighbors remember Powell as a tall, pleasant kid who liked to play stickball and soldier on surrounding streets. To earn money after school, he fixed baby carriages and cribs at a furniture store.

Growing up in an ethnically mixed neighborhood gave Powell a sense of confidence that proved essential when he entered the larger world. He never thought that being a black American was *his* problem. If other people wanted to worry about it, that was their problem. Powell was too busy setting his own goals and working toward them to bother with having a chip on his shoulder.

Ask him who his heroes are, and the husky six-footer still gets tears in his eyes when he talks about his parents, who emigrated from Jamaica. Luther and Maude Powell spoke the King's English with a lilting West Indies accent, and considered themselves British subjects before becoming Americans.

Powell's parents worked in the garment industry. His father was a shipping clerk, and his mother a seamstress who did piecework at home before going down to 34th Street to pick up her pay. They read books and newspapers, had attended school, and repeatedly treated their children to a potent message: education is the single most important ingredient for success in America.

"We came from families who dreamed for you, who demanded achievement, and who believed you must not waste yourself," said Powell's cousin, Grace Watson, remembering their childhood.

Powell was an avid reader and made above-average grades throughout public school. His neighborhood provided plenty of temptation for young people to stray. And like many urban kids today, Powell was exposed to many images of poverty, despair, and drug addiction.

To combat these potential dangers, the Powell children were always closely supervised by their grandmother or their parents' friends after school. One day, when he was about 8, Powell decided to play hooky from school. But the youngster got confused about the time and came home too early. A neighbor who was taking care of the kids caught him — and for a long time after that, he was taken to school and dropped right at the door.

When he was in junior high, Powell had his first taste of leadership after the students elected him captain of their class. He then attended Morris High School, where he received several graduation honors, including a plaque with a doorknob on it to symbolize how education opens doors.

"I didn't know where my future would lie," said Powell, looking back to that day in 1954. "But I know where it all started — the day I got my diploma."

Powell went to college not because he wanted to, but because his parents expected him to. "In those days, when your parents expected something, it was what you had to do," said Powell. "In my family, especially, you did what your parents expected of you."

So at 17, he entered the tuition-free City College of New York. On his parents' advice, Powell chose the School of Engineering. But when an instructor in a mechanical drawing course asked him to visualize a cone intersecting a plane in space, Powell knew he was in the wrong field.

Earlier that spring, he had noticed a bunch of fellows wandering around campus in uniforms. Watching these students, who were part of the ROTC detachment, rekindled his childhood interest in the military. Powell had spent his elementary school years following World War II and his teenage years watching and hearing about the Korean War.

Powell decided to sign up for ROTC and something clicked. He joined the Pershing Rifles, a group that wore special insignia: their uniforms sported red whipcord on the shoulder, which meant the members were part of a fraternity of sorts and in many cases were more serious than average ROTC cadets. A good many made tentative commitments to military careers.

Powell spent the next four years concentrating on ROTC, devoting most of his time to Pershing Rifle activities and often only tolerating the core academics at City College.

In 1958, with a grade average of slightly above *C* (thanks to four years of *A*'s in ROTC), Powell graduated as a cadet colonel and a Pershing Rifles company commander with the designation of "distinguished military graduate." He also received a bachelor of science degree in geology for, as he described it, mastering rock formations under Manhattan.

At 21, he was on his way to the army. Most importantly, he had fulfilled another of his parents' expectations—he had a job.

"In those days, you went to school for the purpose of making yourself employable," said Powell. His parents also expected that their children would surpass them. With all his advantages, Powell has often felt there was no way he could give his own children values and goals equal to the ones he received from his parents.

Looking back on his college days, Powell feels he received a valuable education that gave him an appreciation of the liberal arts, an insight into the fundamentals of government, and a deep respect for the democratic system. Even in later years, when he found himself competing with West Pointers and Ivy Leaguers, he believed his education was so solid that he never regretted going to City College.

171

Colin Powell

But he does regret that ROTC, which gave him his start, was terminated at City College during the Vietnam War resistance. Besides providing students with structure and discipline, he said, it prepared them for an honorable profession that makes a vital contribution to our country.

Powell knows this firsthand. After college, he began a career that took him to the top. His first stop was Infantry Officers Basic Training at Fort Benning. From there, he was shipped to Germany for his first assignment as a platoon leader and company executive officer.

While stationed in Massachusetts, First Lieutenant Powell met his future wife, Alma. They married in 1962. Over their three-decade marriage, she has lived through many scary moments and said plenty of prayers for her soldier husband.

There was the time in Vietnam when Powell was leading a combat unit and stepped on a punji stick. It entered his left sole and came out the top of his foot. Another time he put his own life on the line to save fellow soldiers, whom he pulled from a crashed helicopter that was about to explode.

Powell completed two tours of duty in Vietnam during the sixties. There, he built a growing reputation as a natural born leader.

The next decade was a busy one for Powell. He earned a master's degree in business administration, and was selected as a White House Fellow to serve in the Office of Management and Budget. It was then that he captured the attention of Casper "Cap" Weinberger, who would play an important role as his mentor. When Weinberger later became U.S. Secretary of Defense, he was in a position to bring Powell in to perform top jobs that helped build his career and boost his professional reputation.

"The White House Fellowship experience had a profound impact on my career," Powell said. "What I learned about government as a White House Fellow was the key to the opportunities that came my way. I know of no other program that provides such a learning experience."

After a tour of duty in Korea, Powell returned to the Pentagon, then went on to attend the National War College. In 1979, he became a brigadier general. After receiving the promotion, Powell spent much of his time in Washington advising high-level Pentagon leaders as they directed the armed forces through a number of international crises and the minefields of Pentagon politics. As a White House official, he mediated battles between the State Department and the military.

In 1987, President Reagan asked Powell to serve as National Security Advisor. He became the first black to hold the position. Powell helped the President deal with a number of challenges, including seven summit meetings and the opening of a new era in American-Soviet relations. For the next two years, he was the key advisor for coordinating the activities of the CIA and the State and Defense Departments.

In 1989, Powell's career took quantum leaps. In April, he became a four-star general; in October, President Bush appointed him Chairman of the Joint Chiefs of Staff, making him not only the youngest chairman ever, but also the first black in that position. The chairman acts as the principal military advisor to the President, the Secretary of Defense, and the National Security Council.

The day Powell stood at the podium to be formally recognized as the twelfth chairman, all conversation stopped when, with his characteristic poise and charm, he began to speak of inspiration, family, and young men and women going to war. No one understood the significance of his appointment more keenly than the general himself. He was well aware that in Washington, the highest levels of political power are noticeably white.

In appointing Powell, the nation's official power structure was sending a history-making message: here's a black man who's so respected that he will be admitted to the ultra-exclusive club of global power, that his judgment will be relied upon to determine the safety and future of our nation, and that he will be entrusted with the most guarded secrets of the West.

As a kid in the South Bronx, Powell never dreamed that one day, he would occupy the Pentagon office of the chairman of the Joint Chiefs of Staff. "My ambitions . . . were modest at the time," he recalled. "They were simply to get out of New York, get a job, and go out and have some excitement."

Today Powell and his wife live in the graceful old house reserved for the chairman. It sits atop a hill in Fort Meyer, Virginia, with a grand view of the Potomac River and the city of Washington. The couple, who have raised three children, always made family life a high priority, in spite of the numerous moves Powell's career demanded over the years.

Powell has only one complaint about his position as chairman. He can't pursue his long-time hobby of repairing and rebuilding old cars. "That august place that I live in makes it a little difficult to have old Volvos laying around the yard," he said, grinning. "It drags down the neighborhood."

174

Some people accuse Powell of turning his back on his black heritage and selling out to the white establishment. But nothing is further from the truth. The most gratifying thing about his history-making appointment is the pride it gives the black community and what it means to African-Americans everywhere. Powell said, "It raises the expectation level a little higher."

Besides hard work, Powell attributes his success to Martin Luther King, Jr., who he claims fought the second "Civil War." Powell said the civil rights leader was "instrumental in breaking down barriers to opportunities to such an extent that I've been able to get to where I am." King's example of moral courage continues to influence him, he said.

In spite of his busy schedule, Powell often speaks to young people across the country. Whatever the occasion, his message is always the same: "You must finish high school."

He also offers this advice: set goals and work toward them consistently; avoid drugs; have the courage to face obstacles; and grab the opportunities that come your way.

"There are many more opportunities for you than there were for me," he says.

Whatever your heritage—black, Puerto Rican, or other minority—be proud of who you are, Powell urges. "Most importantly, don't give up.

"If you work hard, if you're well-prepared, if you learn from your failures, and if you always do the very best you can, then your chances of success are increased a hundred times," he says.

Powell impresses upon young people that earning a high school diploma is the first step in achieving dreams. Dropping out only leads to dead ends, he tells them. "In 1954, I got my diploma, and if you get your diploma, you are on your way to somewhere. I am giving you an order—I am a general, you know—I order you to stick with it and get that diploma and stay off drugs."

His talks have encouraged many young people.

Said one listener, Miguel Santiago, "You know he's from the Bronx and you figure, if he could do it, we can do it. I mean he doesn't inspire people just to be soldiers necessarily. He inspires them to be somebody."

Patricia Saiki

> ★ *Our nation has always been the land of opportunity for those willing to aim high, work hard, and be ready to tough it out for the long haul. Short-term "success" is fleeting and illusory. Have patience and be willing to defer quick rewards for the true long-term value.*

What's a girl to do? She might grow up the old-fashioned way and do whatever men tell her to, or she could try Patricia Saiki's approach: do whatever she wants.

The first Asian-American to head the nation's Small Business Administration (SBA), Saiki said she "discovered early on that women had to begin breaking down long-standing traditional barriers in order to achieve even the *chance* to succeed in their chosen careers."

Before launching herself to the top, Saiki had always "assumed opportunities for women were the same as for men." It was an assumption based upon her upbringing.

Born in Hawaii, where Asian-Americans outnumber Caucasians, Saiki didn't have to deal with discrimination as a young girl. Everyone seemed to fit in, because everyone was part of some minority group. But when she reached adulthood in the late forties and early fifties, the simple equality of her childhood was replaced by more complex dynamics. Saiki wasn't just a Japanese descendant anymore—she was a woman facing new expectations, her own and society's.

At the time, nursing, teaching, and secretarial jobs were socially acceptable for women who had to work. But the idea of a woman actually wanting a "man's job"—anything from plumbing to the presidency—was unconventional, even strange. And for a woman to continue working after getting married and having children was interpreted as bad news: it meant her husband couldn't earn enough to support a family. Men were the official breadwinners, the decision-makers, and that was that.

Luckily, Saiki's parents, who were second-generation Japanese-Americans, had prepared their daughter for life's obstacles. Together, they taught her a blend of Japanese and American values: independence, a sense of commitment, pride in one's self and one's work, and family devotion.

"My father encouraged me to become whatever I wanted to become," she said, "and assured me that with hard work and discipline, I could achieve whatever I set my sights on. My mother taught me the basic values of responsibility and productivity, and gave me a clear sense of direction."

So Saiki set her sights high and took off. One of her first stops on the way to political life took her nearly five thousand miles from her hometown of Hilo to Toledo, Ohio, where she taught in a junior high school. Her late husband, a successful Japanese-American doctor, was "supportive every step of the way," she said, and never once felt threatened by her ambitions and accomplishments.

It was the rest of the country that troubled her. When Saiki began her career, most everyone agreed a woman should stretch herself about as far as her kitchen and her clothesline would allow. The "weaker sex" couldn't get mortgages or credit cards; a "thank you" for having a hot meal on the table every evening when the husband returned from work was considered credit enough.

As Saiki encountered this world in which men could easily and legally exclude women, locking them out of high-paying jobs and depriving them of financial freedom, she became more and more frustrated. She wanted change, she wanted action, and she wanted it fast. So after twelve years of teaching, her classroom days became history as she forged ahead into public service.

Back in Hawaii, she became a leading figure in several state and national organizations that supported education and women's rights. She also went political, winning a seat in the Hawaii State House and then in the State Senate. Eventually, after a tough fight, she gained token acceptance as "one of the boys," swinging her golf clubs alongside men and serving on the boards of directors of several Hawaii-based companies.

It was then that she learned how businesses of all sizes worked—

Patricia Saiki

and *didn't* work. She also found out, as the mother of three daughters and two sons, what it took to juggle a family and a career. These firsthand realizations would play a prominent role in Saiki's future.

Her determination to succeed and her conviction that others deserved the same chance pointed Saiki toward Washington, D.C. In 1986, her home district, which was made up of mostly Democrats, voted Saiki, a Republican, into the nation's Congress. There, her personal experiences set her political agenda. Economic issues and child care topped the list.

"Without adequate child care," she said, "the millions of families headed by females who live in poverty cannot hope to break the cycle of despair that grips their lives. As the mother of five children, I know what is involved in trying to raise a family and pursue a professional career. It is not easy, even under the best of circumstances. For most families, the best of circumstances is simply out of reach."

Besides convictions, Saiki came to Congress with style. Bob Wernet, who has known and worked with her since the seventies, described her as a leader with an outgoing nature, who "works quickly, is direct and to the point, demands the best from people— and usually gets what she wants."

But when she doesn't, Saiki relies on her "marvelous sense of humor" to put things in perspective and move on, he said.

In 1991, after Saiki lost a close race for the Senate, President Bush selected her as chief executive officer of the Small Business Administration. With her new post, Saiki inherited a load of problems. At the time, the SBA had a reputation for being a dumping ground for government losers and was regarded by some as a waste of taxpayers' money. Embroiled in scandals, the SBA had been the subject of complaints by minorities, and morale among the agency's five thousand employees was at an all-time low.

What more could a woman who enjoys a good challenge possibly want? In accepting the job, Saiki said she regarded the responsibility as an honor because "small business is the backbone of the American economy."

As for the SBA, she described it as "the agency with the greatest potential." Her first order of business was to create a spirit of optimism and enthusiasm by demonstrating her openness to others' ideas. Using simple but tried-and-true techniques, such as installing suggestion boxes around her headquarters, she began to boost employee morale and enliven the SBA. To pick up the pace even more, she computerized the agency's 110 offices around the country, a move that took the SBA "light years ahead of where it was," Wernet said.

Knowing her way around a golf course, as well as around Con-

179

gress, also proved handy in her efforts to streamline the SBA. A tournament is the perfect opportunity to negotiate business with colleagues.

"That's the time you can take them by the elbow and say, 'Hey, I'm really sorry we couldn't take care of that problem for you, but you know how it is, we all have our jobs to do.'

"It goes down a little easier that way," she explained, "instead of just a 'no' over the phone."

Part of Saiki's agenda at the SBA calls for some not-so-routine work. When tens of thousands of small businesses were looted and burned to the ground during the Los Angeles riots in the spring of 1992, President Bush told her to go out there, assess the damage, and report back. When Saiki completed that assignment, she had to return to California again—this time on Air Force One—to guide the President through the mess.

Just a few months later, when Hurricane Andrew devastated Florida and Louisiana, she quickly boarded a plane, visited the disaster areas, and did whatever she could for the small-business owners who had lost everything.

A powerful and influential policymaker, Saiki's clearly a success at most things she sets her mind to. But she's not about to say "I've made it." Because, as she puts it, "there is always so much more to do. But in striving to achieve, I believe it is very important to enjoy every step of the way, and I've done that."

When she's not jetting around in the line of duty, Saiki is with her family—which could mean just about anywhere in the United States. Between her own homes in Virginia and Hawaii, and her children's homes scattered across the country, Saiki is usually on her way to family gatherings or on the phone arranging the next visit.

And if she had it to do all over again, this woman who has been such an advocate for change probably wouldn't do much to alter the course of her life. "I really don't know whether I would have wanted to do it, or could have done it, differently," Saiki said.

Maria Azucena Vigil

★ | *Reach out your hand to those behind you and bring them up to your side, so the dream will become a reality for all of us. What is important is not to arrive first, but rather, that we all arrive— together and in time.*

As a little girl, Maria Azucena Vigil loved to play "teacher." She would set up a school on her family's back porch and then invite her younger sisters and neighborhood children to be students in her imaginary classroom.

Little did anyone, least of all Vigil, realize that four decades later she would be lauded as an educational pioneer and one of the nation's premier teachers. In 1992, Vigil was named California Teacher of the Year—the latest in a long list of honors saluting her dedication to the profession and her inspired leadership in helping to introduce bilingual education to public schools.

Vigil is a kindergarten teacher at Las Lomas Elementary School in La Habra, California, where almost 70 percent of the students are Hispanic. Many live in poverty with parents who never went beyond grade school and only recently immigrated to the United States. Often these students speak little or no English, and some don't even understand their native tongue well enough to express themselves clearly.

But when they walk into Vigil's classroom, a whole new world opens up to them.

"It is truly a joy to watch her teach her students," said Mary Jo Anderson, the principal of Las Lomas Elementary School.

"Her children learn not only the basics, but how to care for and support each other. I always enjoy my visits to Maria's classroom because I come away with a feeling that 'all will soon be right with the world.' "

181

Colleagues praise not only Vigil's skill, but also the spirit she brings to her profession.

"Maria is like the heartbeat of the best we have to offer our students and their parents," said Richard A. Hermann, superintendent of the La Habra City School District.

"She is always there, ready to support our school system with bursts of energy combined with sustaining surges of enthusiasm, joy, goodwill, and quality. We feel blessed to be touched by the likes of Maria Vigil."

Despite her childhood game, Vigil didn't become a teacher until she was 30—and had already started another kind of life.

"Being a child of my time and culture, I married upon high school graduation," Vigil said. "I was raised to be a hardworking realist. My mother's hope was that her daughters would not have to go to work in a factory—perhaps we might be clerks in a shop or office.

"By the time I was 29, I had seven children," she said. Enjoying motherhood, she was, by her own account, a typical 1950s homemaker: "I cleaned, cooked, sewed, camped, became a Cub Scout den mother, participated in PTA, and helped to teach a catechism class."

At a neighbor's request, she volunteered in a Head Start class. Suddenly her life came full circle. "It was there I found myself again," Vigil said.

Vigil, who's Mexican, had been recruited because many of the students spoke Spanish, but none of the Head Start teachers did. "So I went," Vigil recalled, "and there I saw children who were going through the same things I had gone through as a child, and had forgotten as I became an adult—I mean my children grew up in a middle-class American neighborhood.

"But going back into that classroom and seeing poor children who couldn't speak English, who didn't understand the teacher, who had never been in a school, who were overwhelmed by the whole thing—I identified with them."

Vigil was born in Lego, West Virginia, a company mining town that was home to many immigrants—Hungarians, Italians, Mexicans, and others. Vigil's family lived there until she was 6. But during that time, her grandfather was killed in a mining accident and her father was permanently injured in a mine explosion.

Maria Vigil

Vigil was the oldest of three daughters. Her immigrant parents had only primary educations and spoke no English.

"My sisters and I began school speaking Spanish," Vigil said. "It was then that I began living two very separate lives—two languages, two cultures, two environments."

She was enthralled with both: "School offered a view of middle-class America and holiday traditions, such as Halloween, Thanksgiving, and Valentine's Day. I learned to love songs like 'Home on the Range,' games like London Bridge, and poems like 'Hiawatha.'"

Her home life offered love, but few luxuries.

183

Yet, Vigil has many rich memories of her parents. Her father was a gentle and kind man who loved to read and nourished her hunger for knowledge. "Reading to us daily and taking us on weekly trips to the public library was his legacy to my sisters and to me," Vigil said.

Her mother was a simple woman with a quiet strength that Vigil has come to revere. Vigil was 13 when her father died and her mother moved the family to California to be near relatives. A widow at 32, Vigil's mother supported their family on the $100 a month she earned cleaning houses and cooking for a Latino physician. Vigil appreciates now that much of her life was a "sheer struggle to survive, but she was a proud woman who would never accept charity."

Vigil's mother only spoke limited English, but she did become an American citizen who worked until retirement. "When I think of what my mother did for us," Vigil said, "I feel very humble."

Family, including aunts and uncles, played an important role in Vigil's childhood because "they had such true values — I mean right was right." They taught her the importance of meeting her obligations, accepting responsibility, and respecting her elders.

"I never felt ashamed of being a minority — that never entered my mind," she said. "But I remember feeling ashamed of being poor and hurt when we were going to school — it was the *only* place I felt that," Vigil said.

Even now, the painful memories of her school years are so vivid Vigil must choke back the tears before she can continue.

"I *so wanted* to understand and to be understood," she said. But as a young student, she was "nervous and afraid" of teachers. "When my teachers would smile, I felt good," she said. "When they frowned, I wished I could disappear."

Trying to communicate in two languages was a constant challenge. With parents who didn't speak English and teachers who rarely spoke Spanish, Vigil was left to her own resources. Much of what she knew about English, she picked up simply by listening to other people speak, so the nuances of the language often escaped her.

Until Vigil was in fifth grade she'd only encountered female teachers. Based on her early life in the South, she'd learned to respectfully answer "yes ma'am" whenever they addressed her. That's how she happened to call her school principal "ma'am"—a particularly bad choice since he'd just returned from a tour of duty in World War II.

On that particular day, Vigil had been summoned to the principal's office, along with several other students who had been chosen as hall monitors. To young Vigil, this was an honor and an important responsibility, so she listened carefully as the principal passed out their special badges and instructed them on the duties of a hall monitor.

"He said we were to be like Marines—I'll never forget that—and we were to report even our sisters if they ran, or our best friends, because they were breaking the rules."

When the principal finished laying out the rules, he asked the students, "Do you understand?" And Vigil, who was standing in the front row, obediently answered, "Yes ma'am."

The principal marched over to her. "What did you say?"

She repeated in a loud and clear voice, "Yes ma'am."

That did it. The principal grabbed Vigil and began to shake her violently. "I fell to the floor and everyone was tittering in that nervous giggle that kids get," Vigil recalled. "And then I ran out of the room, crying. But I didn't know what I had done—all I knew was that he was very angry with me."

It was not until many years later, in high school, that she understood what had happened. While reading a bilingual book that featured English on one side of the page and Spanish on the other, Vigil came across the term "sir" for the first time.

"That's when I realized that sir was how you addressed a man," she said. And suddenly that day in the principal's office flashed in her mind. "The principal had thought I was making fun of him," Vigil said. Though nothing could have been further from the truth, the damage was done.

"Sometimes I think teachers tend to think the worst of kids—because he obviously didn't know my predicament," Vigil said.

Memories like that "have made me very sensitive to the hurts that are not children's fault," Vigil said.

After receiving her bachelor's degree from the University of California at Irvine in 1971, Vigil taught her first year of bilingual education in Orange County. So much progress has been made since then, she said. "Twenty years ago, students were forbidden to speak languages other than English in or out of class."

Today, Vigil teaches primarily in Spanish, but she also includes a lesson in English every day to help her students develop the skills they will need as they move into mainstream America.

Vigil believes that the interaction between teacher and pupil sets the foundation for learning—her job is to help students learn, not reprimand them for what they don't know.

"I establish a nurturing environment so that children not only feel successful as students, they also learn to love learning," Vigil said.

Knowing how unsettling it can be to straddle two cultures, she also works hard to make her students feel good about who they are. "I compliment the students, not only for achievement, but for kindness, for responsibility, for their individual interests—even on the historical significance of their names," Vigil said.

"Hispanic names, such as 'Rodrigo,' can be a source of embarrassment for some children, yet how their self-concept and self-esteem are enhanced when they learn that King Rodrigo was a most important historical figure, initiating the reconquest of Spain from the Moors.

"I have seen a simple bit of knowledge such as this encourage many children to say their names with a new sense of pride."

Kids can't fail under Vigil's tutelage. "I display no charts where some students star, but others die," she said. "I find a way to make every student important."

She does the same for parents. Because of her heritage and upbringing, Vigil brings a special insight to her job that goes way beyond simply speaking Spanish in the classroom.

"Maria has been a critical link between the school and parents," said Principal Anderson.

For example, Vigil helped launch a Family Math Program that provides lessons to children and their parents. And when it became apparent that students' grades were suffering because their parents were taking them out of school to go on trips to Mexico, Vigil helped draft a letter to Spanish-speaking parents that explained the importance of planning vacations around the school schedule.

"We had many parents who were just taking off, having their vacations when it was convenient for them—not realizing that taking off at, say, the beginning of December and not coming back until the end of January was a hardship on their children, in terms of their schooling," she said.

Vigil's counsel on such matters is widely sought—not just by parents but by her professional peers—and her wisdom is highly regarded in the Hispanic community.

She takes advantage of every opportunity to educate parents, especially new immigrants, on how they can support their children's education. One such example is a talk she gave at a scholarship ceremony. Vigil not only congratulated the scholarship winners— she coached their parents on how to be supportive of their children's college studies.

Working from a few notes she'd jotted down that morning, Vigil spoke from her heart, delivering a message that switched comfortably back and forth between her two languages: English for the students; Spanish for their parents.

Vigil's bilingual approach ensured that the meaning of her message was not lost. "I wanted the parents to understand that just because their children are 18 years old, they're not through with them—that the next four years are very important and that they still need to continue supporting them," Vigil explained.

She told stories of students who had dropped out of college, or not accepted scholarships, because they felt their families needed them—and the regular paycheck they could contribute to the household income.

And she offered a number of practical parenting tips: be sure your children set aside time to study; don't let the little ones get into their things or destroy their work; if they aren't as helpful as usual around the house, "at times you'll need to forgive them."

Vigil said her advice was guided by the realization that many parents in the audience had never gone beyond grade school, "so they really do not know what their children are going through and the struggles they have as students going to college."

Most importantly, Vigil cautioned the parents to be sensitive to the two cultures their children would be dealing with and to understand that sometimes the values of those cultures would conflict: "Don't ever put them where they have to choose between family and their studies," she told them.

187

She concluded her speech by encouraging the students who had won scholarships to "take every opportunity to make opportunities for your brothers and sisters.

"Reach out your hand to those behind you and bring them up to your side, so that the dream will become a reality for all of us. We have a saying in Spanish: What is important is not to arrive first, but rather, that we all arrive—together and in time."

Vigil's compassionate words of wisdom hit home. After the ceremony, so many people asked for copies of her talk that she had to go home and reconstruct her remarks, made from her simple handwritten outline, into a formal, typed speech.

It's been more than two decades since Vigil, quite by accident, found her calling in life. Her seven children are grown and now she's a grandmother of fifteen. She's weathered a divorce and is happily married for a second time. As for her career, Vigil, now 52, has more than made up for her late start: her six-page, single-spaced résumé is loaded with credentials and awards.

But one thing hasn't changed—Vigil still approaches her teaching with a missionary zeal.

"Teachers touch the future every day," she said. "They must be sensitive, kind, caring, and loving. They must remember to see the world through the eyes of a child.

"I look forward to each day with the enthusiasm and joy that I expect my students to have as they arrive each morning. If I, the teacher, am not interested in having fun, and enjoying the learning experience, how can I possibly expect that of my students?"

Because Vigil loves what she does so much, at times she's inclined to downplay her accomplishments and her contributions. She even jokes that "teaching and gardening are the two most optimistic professions—because you plant something with the hope it will blossom." But without a doubt, being in the classroom is her life's greatest satisfaction, she said.

"I don't think of myself as successful in terms of anything else," she said. "There are many, many more people, and certainly minorities, who have the kinds of careers that I think people admire, such as doctors and lawyers."

Maybe so. But some folks would argue that the world could use a few more Maria Vigils.

All she knows is that she's found the place where she belongs. "Each of us has an optimum role to play in life, according to our talents, experiences, and passions—one role where we, as individuals, can make a significant difference," Vigil said.

"For me, that role is a teacher, working with children. I would do nothing else."

Maxine Waters

★ | *No matter how bad it is, we must be optimistic people will believe in the power of people together and respecting each other. No matter how hard it is, we can never give up. We must always believe it can happen in our lifetime.*

President Bush was holding an invitation-only meeting of congressional leaders and Cabinet members to hash out the tensions that erupted into riots in Los Angeles in the spring of 1992. Suddenly, there was an unexpected knock on the White House door: Representative Maxine Waters, of California's 29th District, where violence had left her own neighborhood in shambles and a nation in shock, was crashing the President's party.

"I don't intend to be excluded or dismissed," she had told a fellow legislator when she learned about the meeting. "We have an awful lot to say."

To no one's surprise, when Waters arrived at his door, the President let her in.

In political circles, Waters, now 54, is serving her first term in Congress, she has earned a reputation as a tough legislator who speaks out loud and clear on her priority issues: women, children, and the American family. But in the wake of the riots, this Democratic congresswoman won her country's ear as never before.

Speaking to groups across the map, appearing on radio and TV talk shows, and suddenly popping up in newsprint everywhere, Waters was both praised and criticized for her unapologetic, empathic feelings about the rioters—her own people. In the midst of the crisis, she was clearly in control. More than any other political figure from L.A., including the city's mayor, Waters got people listening—and it wasn't by being subtle.

"Listen up, America," she told a cheering crowd at a rally in Washington, D.C. "We want to talk to you today. Our children are hurting, our mothers are tired, and our young men are angry."

Waters was speaking from the heart and from firsthand knowledge. She lives within blocks of the area hardest hit by the riots. One of the first problems she discovered when she arrived on the scene of her riot-torn district was a housing development where people were desperately in need of food. So she and her staff dug into their pockets and came up with $250—enough to buy food for all, including milk substitutes for the babies.

Waters's no-nonsense approach goes back to her childhood as the fifth of thirteen children living in a St. Louis, Missouri, housing project.

"We were not taught diplomacy as much as how to fend for ourselves," Waters explained. "To *defend* ourselves is what it really was. You had to make sure you shared in the opportunity, be it dinner or something going on in the family or in the neighborhood."

Growing up in the 1940s and bussing tables at a segregated restaurant when she was 13, Waters had no idea that her aggressive manner was considered "unladylike" or, for that matter, improper for blacks, who were supposed to "know their place." For her, it was simply a way to survive.

Now a fighter for the people she represents—mostly blacks, Hispanics, and other minorities—Waters rose from the ghetto to the halls of government the hard way. She is part of the first "bridge generation" of female politicians, women who have lived two very different—and sometimes conflicting—lives: one in the home, toiling under the kitchen lights, and the other in the public spotlight.

Rather than clashing, though, Waters sees her roles as complementary. Like other women politicians, especially minority women, her politically nontraditional, often controversial, agenda has grown out of her life experiences. African-American female officeholders, in particular, typically earn credibility and build essential political skills as community leaders, as church leaders, and as heads of families often lacking significant male leadership and support.

Waters's path to political power was clearly influenced by the circumstances of her life, first in Missouri and later in California.

Waters and her family moved to California in 1961. There she

Maxine Waters

worked in a garment factory, raised her two children, eventually divorced, and later earned her bachelor's degree in sociology at California State University at Los Angeles.

After the 1965 Watts riots, another of L.A.'s racial outbursts, she became an assistant teacher for the Head Start program. During that period, she also began to build her political skills by campaigning for local and state politicians. Then in 1976, she made her own political bid, winning a seat to the state Assembly.

As a freshman politician, Waters pursued her agenda with a passion. She soon became known as "the conscience" of the California legislature. She also is credited with engineering the speakership of Willie Brown. The two became such close colleagues and influential forces that in political circles, they were known as "Moses" and "Mosetta." Even in this bond, Waters distinguished herself: Brown's irreverent and domineering style reportedly has rattled many a California politician, for when the speaker of the California Assembly speaks, words shoot from his lips like bullets from an Uzi.

But Waters has seemed bulletproof from the start. "I have not attempted to be liked by my male colleagues or to pamper them," she said. "I have not tried to be male enough for them to like me. I simply am what I am; I care about what I care about. *I'm me!* So I've had fights and I've had good moments."

Her good moments in the Assembly include forcing approval of amendments forbidding state pension investments in companies doing business in South Africa, passing minority and women's tenants' rights laws, and setting limits on police searches.

Another special moment took place after hours, when she met her second husband, Sidney Williams, a former pro football player with the Cleveland Browns and now a Mercedes-Benz salesman in Hollywood.

A supportive partner, Williams is clearly comfortable with his wife's power and fame. "I have my career and she has hers," he said. "I'm an ex–professional football player. So all the accolades she's getting, I've gone through. So it's not a big deal. It's her time to be the shining light. She has worked very hard to be in the position that she's in. I enjoy every minute that she's happy."

Even so, public life can put a strain on any marriage. And Waters candidly shares that she and her husband have to sit down and "work on it all the time."

Happy with her marriage, Waters wasn't completely happy with her career: her power was limited to California, but her ideas had no limits.

"Over the years," she recalled, "I've had to ask myself, 'Where do I go from here?' I decided that I wanted to serve in the United States Congress. It was a logical next step career-wise."

Others had doubts. "When I first met Maxine Waters," Representative Charles E. Schumer of Brooklyn recalled, "I assumed she would be the classic outsider, attacking the system and not getting things done internally." But after serving with her on the House of Representatives' Banking, Finance, and Urban Affairs Committee, he said he's been "surprised at what an effective insider she's been. She has a great deal of passion, and is very angry because of the lot that has been dealt her constituents. But she also studies the issues and is willing to work to get things done."

Another fan is Representative Joseph P. Kennedy II of Boston. "Maxine is a breath of fresh air," he said. "She's obviously a very controversial figure because she has a tendency to make people very, very uncomfortable." But, he added, sometimes that's just what a situation calls for.

Stories of Waters's unconventional style abound. That's why the staff of U.S. Speaker of the House Tom Foley was "startled, but not surprised," when this freshman congresswoman bucked political custom by striding into his office and announcing: "I need one hot minute with the speaker!"

Coming from a poor background herself, Waters believes strongly in federal aid for the poor and in affirmative action. She's also big on so-called "women's issues," such as abortion rights legislation, and she denounced the Persian Gulf War, saying that combat is "an obsolete means of resolving conflict."

And, unlike most politicians, she votes her own mind. She neither takes opinion polls nor allows them to sway her vote.

Ever the nonconformist, Waters said, "I don't legislate that way. I try to let people know who I am all the time so they will understand where I'm coming from on issues. I don't pull very many surprises. I think people voted for me because they kind of liked where I was coming from."

Nowhere is that more true than in her home district. The day after the L.A. riots broke out, Waters left her Washington office and boarded a California-bound plane. Looking over her city's devastation—the spoiled food, the looted and burned stores, the loss of electricity—Waters didn't bother knocking on any doors. She simply marched straight into the Department of Water and Power. A few hours and a few angry phone calls later, lights were back on, and hungry mouths had been fed, thanks to the determined efforts of Waters and her staff.

Grateful residents of a housing project cheered and hugged Waters as if she were a superstar. She had brought hope and achieved what seemed impossible in the chaotic aftermath of the violence.

But Waters is the first to point out there's no magic in that kind of miracle-working. "You know what?" she said. "All government systems work the same: the squeaky wheel gets the oil."

Oprah Winfrey

★ | *Just tell the truth. It'll save you every time.*

Like the guests who appear on her television show, Oprah Winfrey put her intimate secrets out there for everyone to know. Hovering between information and titillation, *The Oprah Winfrey Show,* with its seventeen million viewers every weekday afternoon, is television at the outer limits.

"I'm a truth seeker," said Winfrey. "That's what I do every day on the show—put out the truth. Some people don't like it, they call it sensationalism, but I say life is sensational."

That attitude, plus her animated delivery, make Winfrey a TV natural. Like most talk show hosts, she's inquisitive—it's her job to ask lots of questions and probe the thoughts and feelings of her guests. But audiences agree that the way Winfrey handles sensitive subjects sets her apart.

Something magical happens when she holds a mike in her right hand and reaches out her left to a guest, often in a sisterly embrace that is at once comforting and coaxing. Winfrey has a knack for wooing people into conversation that verges on confession.

"I believe that good communicative television should be a give and take," Winfrey said. "You give something to the audience and they give back to you. So I expect my audience and my guests to be as open as I am.

"What I have learned in my life and in my work is that the more I am able to be myself, the more it enables other people to be themselves. That is why people tell me things on the air that they have not been able to tell their mother, their daughter, their brother."

Off camera, Winfrey's life is equally dramatic. With large almond-shaped eyes framed by lots of makeup, Winfrey, 37, dresses in bold colors and earrings that make a statement. She's a study in perpetual motion, because inside there's a lot making her tick.

She's more than a black woman who's made it in the white man's world of network TV. More than the star of her own rags-to-riches tale. And more than a survivor—of incest, attempted suicide, and an insecurity that grew out of bouncing through childhood between two parents and a grandmother.

Winfrey's birth is a story that could have come straight from one of her shows: her parents never married—she was the product of a furlough romance in Mississippi. Soldier Vernon Winfrey, home on leave from the army, returned to active duty unaware that nine months later he'd be a dad. He found out only after Vernita Lee sent him a card announcing their daughter's arrival and asking for baby clothes.

In 1954, work was hard to come by in the small town of Kosciusko, where Winfrey was born, so her mother headed for Milwaukee, Wisconsin, in search of a good-paying job. Baby Oprah was left in the care of her grandmother, on her father's side of the family.

Grandmother Winfrey was a woman of strong character and religious beliefs. She lived by the Bible. Much of Oprah's early life was spent at church, which gave her opportunities to display her talents. By age 3, she was performing in Christmas and Easter pageants. She had a way with words and learned how to read exceptionally well.

Although Grandmother Winfrey appreciated the church performances, at home she wanted her outgoing granddaughter to be seen and not heard. Surrounded by adults, but longing for youthful activity and attention, Oprah began acting up.

By age 6, she wanted to be white. She slept with a clothespin on her nose and prayed for corkscrew curls, because she felt being white would save her from spankings. Though Winfrey knew what her grandmother expected, she remained highly spirited. She could not be controlled, and her grandmother was unbending. Clearly something had to be done.

So Winfrey's mother invited her to come live in Milwaukee, an opportunity the young girl grabbed. But she soon learned that semi-rural life in Mississippi had its advantages over the mean streets of Milwaukee: her mother lived in one room, worked long hours, and had little time for a daughter.

The combined experiences of becoming a mother at a young age and then leaving her baby hadn't prepared Lee for the responsibilities involved in caring for a child. Even with her welfare check, plus her wages as a maid, she couldn't afford much for her daughter. Aimless and unable to pay for simple pleasures, such as movies, young Winfrey turned rebellious and soon became more than her mother could handle.

Now it was Vernon Winfrey's turn to raise his daughter. By then, he had left the army and was living in Nashville, Tennessee. He and his wife welcomed the twelve-year-old into their home. The couple wanted the best for Winfrey, who soon learned they couldn't be worn down as easily as her mother and grandmother. Her new parents put structure in her life. Although Winfrey could read and write well, she was weak in math; they made her study to improve. Her father, who was as religious as his mother, took Winfrey to church, where she again had an opportunity to perform in pageants and chorus.

The following summer, her mother wanted Winfrey to visit; reluctantly, her father let her go. Once in Milwaukee, the girl was convinced to stay after her mother promised things would be better than before. Lee soon married, expanding the family with her new husband's son and daughter.

Winfrey's father was heartbroken at the arrangement, knowing his daughter would not receive the support and discipline she needed. His worst fears were realized; the return to Milwaukee left Winfrey with scars that would be hard to heal.

As a teenager, Winfrey again became concerned with her skin color. She needed her mother's attention, but instead felt cast off by everyone at home. She became convinced that she was neglected in favor of her light-skinned stepsister.

To forget her pain, Winfrey lost herself in books. Stuck in a family that had no respect for reading, intelligence, or school, Winfrey grew more angry and isolated. She concluded, based on the many moves back and forth between her parents, that neither of them really loved her.

During this period, and when living with her mother earlier, Winfrey said, she was the victim of sexual abuse by male family members and friends. "It happened over a period of years between 9 and 14,"

Oprah Winfrey

she said. "I remember blaming myself for it, thinking something must be wrong with me." Confused and frightened, she never told anyone about the attacks.

Despite her troubled life, Winfrey continued to be a good student. A teacher helped her get a scholarship to a prestigious school in an affluent area. But her achievements were clouded by emotional outbreaks. On several occasions, Winfrey destroyed family belongings, then pretended their apartment had been burglarized. Twice she ran away. And she was nearly sent to a detention home. Overwhelmed by these events, Winfrey's mother sent her back to her father.

It was a vastly different girl who returned to Nashville. At 14, she was far too worldly for her years. Her strong-willed father took charge, setting high standards for conduct and achievement—and making sure Winfrey met them. At the time, he was a barber and also owned a grocery store. "I had to work in the store," Winfrey said, "and I hated it, every minute of it. Hated it. Selling penny candy, Popsicles. But without him—even with all of this potential—I never would have blossomed."

In high school, she excelled at public speaking and dramatics. Senior year was an exciting time for Winfrey, who dreamed of a career in the performing arts. Among her many achievements, she attended the 1970 White House Conference on Youth in Washington. On a trip to Los Angeles to speak at a church, she toured Hollywood. The local black radio station in Nashville, WVOL, hired her to read the news. And she became "Miss Black Tennessee."

"I won on poise and talent," said Winfrey, adding that the experience proved that being dark-skinned didn't matter when it came to being the best and smartest.

She hoped to leave home for college, but her father decided she should attend Tennessee State University in Nashville. There she won a scholarship in a speaking contest and majored in language arts.

Continuing as a news announcer at WVOL, she was soon hired by a major radio station, WLAC. Before long, she moved to WLAC-TV as a reporter-anchor. Even though Winfrey was earning a five-figure salary while she attended college, her father continued to be as strict as ever. Frustrated that he still enforced a midnight curfew, Winfrey landed a job in Baltimore at WJZ-TV—and left Nashville without completing her degree.

Winfrey was in for a shock at her new job when the station insisted on changing her appearance. "They told me my nose was too wide, my hair too thick and long, and they sent me to a place in New York to get my first perm," she said.

She had embarked on her broadcasting career with very little formal training in journalism. Her reporting was not objective and she didn't follow direction, preferring instead to handle stories emotionally. But since she'd signed a solid contract, Winfrey couldn't be fired, so management had to find a better use for her talents.

They made her co-host of a local morning show, *People Are Talking,* which ran in competition with *Donahue.* Suddenly the subjective quality that had undermined Winfrey's reporting became a strength. She was a stimulating interviewer and her engaging personality and genuine style were a big hit with audiences.

The spirited Winfrey had found her niche. The show's producer, Sherry Burns, said of her, "Oprah is a wonderful, wonderful person. Who she is on-camera is exactly what she is off-camera. She's a totally approachable, real, warm person."

Although Winfrey was attractive, slim, and earning more than $100,000 a year in Baltimore, old insecurities haunted her. "I had so much going for me, but I still thought I was nothing without a man," said Winfrey, referring to a four-year relationship with a boyfriend who continually rejected her. She felt depleted and powerless without him, and once stayed in bed for three days, missing work.

She even attempted suicide. "Sad, ain't it?" she said, recalling the incident that she now understands was a wake-up call for help. But at the time, she refused to go for counseling; she insisted on being her own person. By herself, she came to the realization that she was being emotionally abused—which can be as damaging as a beating.

"You're not getting knocked around physically, but in terms of your ability to soar, your wings are clipped," she said, describing women who lose themselves in relationships with men. She swore she would never do that again—and she never did.

Once past that crisis, Winfrey also realized she was ready to move to the big time in broadcasting. She sent tapes of her show to TV stations, landing a job as host on *A.M. Chicago* at WLS-TV. The ABC-affiliate aired its show opposite Phil Donahue's, so once again she was competing with the talk show king.

Winfrey immersed herself in her new show, blending earthiness, humor, spontaneity, and candor, with a personal touch. On a program about incest, she impulsively put her arms around the woman speaking and, weeping with her, confided that she too had been sexually abused as a child.

In no time, Winfrey so overshadowed her competition, that the

201

Donahue show retreated to New York. She created such a sensation that *A.M. Chicago* was renamed *The Oprah Winfrey Show.* The move made Winfrey the first black woman to host her own nationally syndicated show.

In 1985, she took a leave of absence from the show to play Sofia in the movie version of Alice Walker's novel *The Color Purple.* Her performance was so powerful that she received an Academy Award nomination. A year later, she appeared in the motion picture *Native Son,* based on Richard Wright's novel. But whatever additional projects Winfrey has taken on in the pursuit of her many career dreams, she remains first and foremost a talk show host.

Included in Winfrey's walk up the mountain of success is the courage to do what no other woman of her professional stature has ever done — go public with her weight. Those who watch her show regularly have seen Winfrey gain and lose multiple dress sizes, her weight swinging as much as seventy pounds.

Winfrey admits her weight is a way of staying comfortable with other people — but it is also a barrier to better things. "So I dream of walking into a room one day where this fat is not an issue," she said. Besides a career that takes her to restaurants at least once a day, Winfrey is caught in a quandary that many share: she loves good food as much as she'd like to lose weight.

Today Winfrey's weeks fall into a pattern. Monday through Wednesday, she arrives at 6 A.M. to work out in the studio's gym. Then she has her hair and makeup done for a 9 A.M. taping; after a production meeting, she tapes a second show at 11. After lunch, it's more production meetings. Thursdays are reserved for paperwork. Friday through Sunday, she's at her 160-acre farm in Indiana, where she relaxes, reads scripts, and meets with producers.

Remembering what it's like to be called into the boss's office, Winfrey always tries to be fair with her employees. She is considered a sister by many. Said one: "We are not structured like a typical Hollywood company. Oprah is very hands-on."

Like most talk show hosts, Winfrey owns her show, and has complete control over it. But unlike others, her company, Harpo Productions (Oprah spelled backward), also owns the large TV and movie studio in Chicago where the show is taped. Winfrey is the first black woman to own a movie-production studio; and after Mary

Pickford and Lucille Ball, only the third female studio owner ever.

"I run this company based on instinct," said Winfrey, who never took a business course. She has been brilliant at creating a public personality and then building an organization to maximize her image. Her hard work has paid off: *The Oprah Winfrey Show* is the highest-ranked talk show in the history of television. The show is broadcast in most U.S. cities and fifty-five countries. Its success has made Winfrey very wealthy—she is estimated by one business magazine to be the country's second-highest-paid entertainer, earning about $88 million in 1991 and 1992.

But when Winfrey first made money, she spent it as fast as it came in. Now that she's a millionaire, she's cut up her charge cards so she doesn't blow her hard-earned dollars on silly things.

"Before, if I couldn't decide which of two dresses I wanted, I bought both of them," she said. "Now if I don't have the cash, I don't buy it. And when you have to count out five hundred dollars in bills, it makes you stop and think."

Mindful of how stern love once saved her, Winfrey and the women on her staff have formed a "Big Sister" group with two dozen teenage girls from a Chicago project where drugs and crime are prevalent. Winfrey invites the teens to her place for pajama parties, and takes them to plays and social gatherings. But she also gives them dictionaries with orders to learn five new words a day. Most of all, she lays down Oprah's Law.

"I shoot a very straight shot," Winfrey said. "Get pregnant, and I'll break your face!"

She talks to the girls about goals. They say they want Cadillacs. She gives them the facts of life.

"If you cannot talk correctly, if you cannot read or do math, if you become pregnant, if you drop out of school, you will never have a Cadillac, I guarantee it! And if you get D's and F's on your report card, you're out of this group. Don't tell me you want to do great things in your life if all you carry to school is a radio!"

The community-minded Winfrey speaks to numerous youth groups, urging listeners to be achievers. She encourages kids to be everything they can be. She also seeks to raise the confidence and self-esteem of female listeners of all ages. Her goal is to help women be independent and free.

Winfrey's elegant condominium apartment in Chicago speaks well of not depending on a man. With marble floors and four baths—including one with a gold swan as the tub faucet, and another with an adjoining sauna—it's a quantum leap from life in a Milwaukee project.

"I don't think of myself as a poor, deprived ghetto girl who made good," said Winfrey. "I think of myself as somebody who from an early age knew I was responsible for myself, and I had to make good."

She enjoys sharing her success. As an employer, she can be extremely generous; as a friend, insanely so. One Christmas she gave each of her eight producers $10,000 and an all-expenses-paid-trip anywhere in the world. As a maid of honor, Winfrey once paid for the wedding and gave the bride pearl-and-diamond earrings, plus a two-week honeymoon on the French Riviera.

By her own account, the past few years have been terrific for Winfrey. Her life isn't perfect. She isn't perfect. She never claimed to be. Yet she feels truly blessed.

"But I also believe that you tend to create your own blessings," she said. "You have to prepare yourself so that when that time comes, you're ready."

She doesn't think success is as difficult as some people make it out to be. It boils down to setting goals and working toward them. And she enjoys that process.

"My main concern about myself now is whether I will live up to my potential. I still sense that the best is yet to to be."

Winfrey's self-assuredness has been hard won—from her chaotic childhood to the ups and downs of her very public career, nothing has been able to break her spirit.

"The more you praise and celebrate your life, the more there is in life to celebrate," she said. "The more you complain, the more you find fault—the more misery and fault you will have to find.

"I am so glad that I did not have to wait until I was 52 to figure this out, to understand the law of cause and effect—that divine reciprocity, reaping what you sow, is the absolute truth."

About the Author

As an NFL All-Pro, Rosey Grier was considered among the most powerful and feared players—a quarterback's terror. Now, with equally fierce determination, he's tackling the crisis in America's inner cities.

An ordained Christian minister, Grier heads "Are You Committed?," a not-for-profit organization that is targeting the problems—crime, unemployment, drugs, single parenthood, and racism, to name a few—that undermine urban communities and threaten the futures of their young people.

AYC is founded on the philosophy that the only way to save communities is to teach people how to help themselves. To that end, the organization is developing a program to launch new businesses in inner cities—businesses that are owned not by absentee entrepreneurs but by people who live in the neighborhood. This strategy will not only provide new jobs, but also shift the economics so that inner cities evolve into communities where young people are surrounded by positive role models—from the store owner around the corner, to their family physician at the neighborhood clinic, to the minister of their local church.

Focusing on solutions with a lasting impact, AYC hopes to achieve its vision through collaboration with business leaders, service agencies, and community organizations dedicated to helping young people become productive members of society.

A model AYC program currently is being developed in Kansas City, Missouri. Grier divides his time between Missouri and southern California.

Long recognized as a social activist with a special interest in the elderly and troubled youth, Grier has received many national awards for his work with America's disadvantaged. His efforts have been recognized and honored with numerous invitations to the White House by several U.S. Presidents.

But Grier is probably best known as a football superstar. He began his professional career with the New York Giants in 1955, after graduating from Penn State.

As an All-Pro defensive tackle, he was coached by the legendary Tom Landry. He was in five NFL championship games before he was traded to the Los Angeles Rams, where he made football history as a member of the "Fearsome Foursome."

After retiring from football in 1968, Grier became one of the first professional athletes to make the transition to television. He has been a guest star in more than seventy television roles and appeared in ten movies.

A talented singer, Grier has performed at Carnegie Hall, as well as other prestigious concert halls and cabarets across the country. Among his musical accomplishments is a children's song called "It's All Right to Cry."

Grier has just completed his first novel, a story about family life in the ghetto, scheduled for publication in 1993.

Additional copies of *Rosey Grier's All-American Heroes* may be ordered for $9.95, plus postage and handling: $2 for the first copy, $1 for each additional copy. Send a check to:

MasterMedia Limited
17 East 89th Street
New York, NY 10128
(212) 260-5600
(800) 334-8232
fax: (212) 546-7607

Rosey Grier is available for speeches and seminars. Please contact MasterMedia's Speakers' Bureau for availability and fee arrangements. Call Tony Colao at (800) 4-LECTUR, or fax: (908) 359-1647.

Other MasterMedia Books

THE PREGNANCY AND MOTHERHOOD DIARY: Planning the First Year of Your Second Career, by Susan Schiffer Stautberg, is the first and only undated appointment diary that shows how to manage pregnancy and career. ($12.95 spiral-bound)

CITIES OF OPPORTUNITY: Finding the Best Place to Work, Live and Prosper in the 1990's and Beyond, by Dr. John Tepper Marlin, explores the job and living options for the next decade and into the next century. This consumer guide and handbook, written by one of the world's experts on cities, selects and features forty-six American cities and metropolitan areas. ($13.95 paper, $24.95 cloth)

THE DOLLARS AND SENSE OF DIVORCE, by Dr. Judith Briles, is the first book to combine practical tips on overcoming the legal hurdles by planning finances before, during, and after divorce. ($10.95 paper)

OUT THE ORGANIZATION: New Career Opportunities for the 1990s, by Robert and Madeleine Swain, is written for the millions of Americans whose jobs are no longer safe, whose companies are not loyal, and who face futures of uncertainty. It gives advice on finding a new job or starting your own business. ($12.95 paper)

AGING PARENTS AND YOU: A Complete Handbook to Help You Help Your Elders Maintain a Healthy, Productive and Independent Life, by Eugenia Anderson-Ellis, is a complete guide to providing care to aging relatives. It gives practical advice and resources to the adults who are helping their elders lead productive and independent lives. Revised and updated. ($9.95 paper)

CRITICISM IN YOUR LIFE: How to Give It, How to Take It, How to Make It Work for You, by Dr. Deborah Bright, offers practical advice, in an upbeat, readable, and realistic fashion, for turning criticism into control. Charts and diagrams guide the reader into managing criticism from bosses, spouses, children, friends, neighbors, in-laws, and business relations. ($17.95 cloth)

BEYOND SUCCESS: How Volunteer Service Can Help You Begin Making a Life Instead of Just a Living, by John F. Raynolds III and Eleanor Raynolds, C.B.E., is a unique how-to book targeted at business and professional people considering volunteer work, senior citizens who wish to fill leisure time meaningfully, and students trying out various career options. The book is filled with interviews with celebrities, CEOs, and average citizens who talk about the benefits of service work. ($19.95 cloth)

MANAGING IT ALL: Time-Saving Ideas for Career, Family, Relationships, and Self, by Beverly Benz Treuille and Susan Schiffer Stautberg, is written for women who are juggling careers and families. Over two hundred career women (ranging from a TV anchorwoman to an investment banker) were interviewed. The book contains many humorous anecdotes on saving time and improving the quality of life for self and family. ($9.95 paper)

YOUR HEALTHY BODY, YOUR HEALTHY LIFE: How to Take Control of Your Medical Destiny, by Donald B. Louria, M.D., provides precise advice and strategies that will help you to live a long and healthy life. Learn also about nutrition, exercise, vitamins, and medication, as well as how to control risk factors for major diseases. Revised and updated. ($12.95 paper)

THE CONFIDENCE FACTOR: How Self-Esteem Can Change Your Life, by Dr. Judith Briles, is based on a nationwide survey of six thousand men and women. Briles explores why women so often feel a lack of self-confidence and have a poor opinion of themselves. She offers step-by-step advice on becoming the person you want to be. ($9.95 paper, $18.95 cloth)

THE SOLUTION TO POLLUTION: 101 Things You Can Do to Clean Up Your Environment, by Laurence Sombke, offers step-by-step techniques on how to conserve more energy, start a recycling center, choose biodegradable products, and even proceed with individual environmental cleanup projects. ($7.95 paper)

TAKING CONTROL OF YOUR LIFE: The Secrets of Successful Enterprising Women, by Gail Blanke and Kathleen Walas, is based on the authors' professional experience with Avon Products' Women of Enterprise Awards, given each year to outstanding women entrepreneurs. The authors offer a specific plan to help you gain control over your life, and include business tips and quizzes as well as beauty and lifestyle information. ($17.95 cloth)

SIDE-BY-SIDE STRATEGIES: How Two-Career Couples Can Thrive in the Nineties, by Jane Hershey Cuozzo and S. Diane Graham, describes how two-career couples can learn the difference between competing with a spouse and becoming a supportive power partner. Published in hardcover as *Power Partners.* ($10.95 paper, $19.95 cloth)

DARE TO CONFRONT! How to Intervene When Someone You Care About Has an Alcohol or Drug Problem, by Bob Wright and Deborah George Wright, shows the reader how to use the step-by-step methods of professional interventionists to motivate drug-dependent people to accept the help they need. ($17.95 cloth)

WORK WITH ME! How to Make the Most of Office Support Staff, by Betsy Lazary, shows you how to find, train, and nurture the "perfect" assistant and how to best utilize your support staff professionals. ($9.95 paper)

MANN FOR ALL SEASONS: Wit and Wisdom from The Washington Post*'s Judy Mann,* by Judy Mann, shows the columnist at her best as she writes about women, families, and the impact and politics of the women's revolution. ($9.95 paper, $19.95 cloth)

THE SOLUTION TO POLLUTION IN THE WORKPLACE, by Laurence Sombke, Terry M. Robertson and Elliot M. Kaplan, supplies employees with everything they need to know about cleaning up their workspace, including recycling, using energy efficiently, conserving water and buying recycled products and nontoxic supplies. ($9.95 paper)

THE ENVIRONMENTAL GARDENER: The Solution to Pollution for Lawns and Gardens, by Laurence Sombke, focuses on what each of us can do to protect our endangered plant life. A practical sourcebook and shopping guide. ($8.95 paper)

THE LOYALTY FACTOR: Building Trust in Today's Workplace, by Carol Kinsey Goman, Ph.D., offers techniques for restoring commitment and loyalty in the workplace. ($9.95 paper)

DARE TO CHANGE YOUR JOB—AND YOUR LIFE, by Carole Kanchier, Ph.D., provides a look at career growth and development throughout the life cycle. ($9.95 paper)

MISS AMERICA: In Pursuit of the Crown, by Ann-Marie Bivans, is an authorized guidebook to the Pageant, containing eyewitness accounts, complete historical data, and a realistic look at the trials and triumphs of the potential Miss Americas. ($19.95 paper, $27.50 cloth)

POSITIVELY OUTRAGEOUS SERVICE: New and Easy Ways to Win Customers for Life, by T. Scott Gross, identifies what the consumers of the nineties really want and how businesses can develop effective marketing strategies to answer those needs. ($14.95 paper)

BREATHING SPACE: Living and Working at a Comfortable Pace in a Sped-Up Society, by Jeff Davidson, helps readers to handle information and activity overload, and gain greater control over their lives. ($10.95 paper)

TWENTYSOMETHING: Managing and Motivating Today's New Work Force, by Lawrence J. Bradford, Ph.D., and Claire Raines, M.A., examines the work orientation of the younger generation, offering managers in businesses of all kinds a practical guide to better understand and supervise their young employees. ($22.95 cloth)

REAL LIFE 101: The Graduate's Guide to Survival, by Susan Kleinman, supplies welcome advice to those facing "real life" for the first time, focusing on work, money, health, and how to deal with freedom and responsibility. ($9.95 paper)

BALANCING ACTS! Juggling Love, Work, Family, and Recreation, by Susan Schiffer Stautberg and Marcia L. Worthing, provides strategies to achieve a balanced life by reordering priorities and setting realistic goals. ($12.95 paper)

REAL BEAUTY . . . REAL WOMEN: A Handbook for Making the Best of Your Own Good Looks, by Kathleen Walas, International Beauty and Fashion Director of Avon Products, offers expert advice on beauty and fashion to women of all ages and ethnic backgrounds. ($19.50 paper)

THE LIVING HEART BRAND NAME SHOPPER'S GUIDE, by Michael E. De-Bakey, M.D., Antonio M. Gotto, Jr., M.D., D.Phil., Lynne W. Scott, M.A., R.D./L.D., and John P. Foreyt, Ph.D., lists brand-name supermarket products that are low in fat, saturated fatty acids, and cholesterol. ($12.50 paper)

MANAGING YOUR CHILD'S DIABETES, by Robert Wood Johnson IV, Sale Johnson, Casey Johnson, and Susan Kleinman, brings help to families trying to understand diabetes and control its effects. ($10.95 paper)

STEP FORWARD: Sexual Harassment in the Workplace, What You Need to Know, by Susan L. Webb, presents the facts for dealing with sexual harassment on the job. ($9.95 paper)

A TEEN'S GUIDE TO BUSINESS: The Secrets to a Successful Enterprise, by Linda Menzies, Oren S. Jenkins, and Rickell R. Fisher, provides solid information about starting your own business or working for one. ($7.95 paper)

GLORIOUS ROOTS: Recipes for Healthy, Tasty Vegetables, by Laurence Sombke, celebrates the taste, texture, and versatility of root vegetables. Contains recipes for appetizers, soups, stews, and baked, broiled, and stir-fried dishes—even desserts. ($12.95 paper)

THE OUTDOOR WOMAN: A Handbook to Adventure, by Patricia Hubbard and Stan Wass, details the lives of adventurous outdoor women and offers their ideas on how you can incorporate exciting outdoor experiences into your life. ($14.95 paper)

FLIGHT PLAN FOR LIVING: The Art of Self-Encouragement, by Patrick O'Dooley, is a life guide organized like a pilot's flight checklist, which ensures you'll be flying "clear on top" throughout your life. ($17.95 cloth)

HOW TO GET WHAT YOU WANT FROM ALMOST ANYBODY, by T. Scott Gross, shows how to get great service, negotiate better prices, and always get what you pay for. ($9.95 paper)

FINANCIAL SAVVY FOR WOMEN: A Money Book for Women of All Ages, by Dr. Judith Briles, divides a woman's monetary lifespan into six phases, discusses the specific areas to be addressed at each stage, and demonstrates how to create a sound lifelong money game plan. ($14.95 paper)

TEAMBUILT: Making Teamwork Work, by Mark Sanborn, teaches business how to improve productivity, without increasing resources or expenses, by building teamwork among employers. ($19.95 cloth)

THE BIG APPLE BUSINESS AND PLEASURE GUIDE: 501 Ways to Work Smarter, Play Harder, and Live Better in New York City, by Muriel Siebert and Susan Kleinman, offers visitors and New Yorkers alike advice on how to do business in the city as well as how to enjoy its attractions. ($9.95 paper)

MIND YOUR OWN BUSINESS: And Keep It in the Family, by Marcy Syms, COO of Syms Corporation, is an effective guide for any organization, small or large, facing what is documented to be the toughest step in managing a family business—making the transition to the new generation. ($18.95 cloth)

KIDS WHO MAKE A DIFFERENCE, by Joyce M. Roché and Marie Rodriguez, is a surprizing and inspiring document of some of today's toughest challenges being met—by teenagers and kids! Their courage and creativity allowed them to find practical solutions. ($8.95 paper; with photos)